Never
Before
Noon

Never Before Noon

AN AUTOBIOGRAPHY

Afdera Fonda

with Clifford Thurlow

WEIDENFELD & NICOLSON
New York

IO TO MIO AND IO . . . AND MAX

Published by Weidenfeld & Nicolson, New York
A Division of Wheatland Corporation
10 East 53rd Street
New York, NY 10022

Originally published in Great Britain by George
Weidenfeld & Nicolson Limited.

Library of Congress Cataloging-in-Publication Data

Fonda, Afdera.
   Never before noon.

   1. Fonda, Henry, 1905– . 2. Actors—United
States—Biography. 3.Fonda, Afdera. 4. Wives—
United States—Biography. I. Title.
PN2287.F558F64 1987 791.43′028′0924 [B] 86–13297
ISBN 1–55584–026–4

First American Edition 1987

10 9 8 7 6 5 4 3 2 1

Contents

Illustrations

Showing a model what shot was wanted, San Giorgio, Venice
With Italian film director Luchino Visconti
With Gianni Agnelli and Sonny Marlborough
With Harry Cubitt
A portrait of Harry at a party
At the Summer Palace in Peking
With John Bailey on Bali
A photograph of me by John Bailey
With Peter Thorneycroft, President Pertini and Charles Forte
At a wedding with the Hambleden lads
The Bridge of Sighs, Venice

All photographs are from the author's collection

Preface

It was a clear, airless day. The entire household, in contrast, was humming and wild-eyed with the news: 'Papa's coming, Papa's coming,' an event that to me meant nothing at all. I was a child of barely three years and his visits were so brief and rare, I wasn't exactly sure who Papa was.

The frivolous mood had changed and become tense and expectant, a small echo of the world outside in that long hot summer of 1936. There were endless warplanes in the sky. Soldiers marched in rigid columns. Mussolini's iron-ringing speeches had followed us from the baked and gossipy streets of Venice to the seaside retreat at Sestri Levante, a journey made every year with nannies and a cluster of fussing servants. I sat in the centre of the floor, hugging my long white dress over my knees and staring at the antics of my brother and two older sisters. They were strutting around the room in the tailored black uniforms of the Fascists, my mother being a chameleon in everything political.

The summer house was a gloomy, pre-Raphaelite villa with a walled courtyard and a maze of small chambers where you could imagine people dying – and, in fact, an elderly housekeeper was dying of cancer and lay ancient and motionless in one of the dark wings. It was a peculiar building that must have been designed by a madman, his great folly being to site the drawing-room at the top of a steep flight of stairs.

The little soldiers became still and the servants stood to attention.

'He's here,' somebody whispered.

I looked down the stairs and he appeared, a towering giant, two metres and more, who climbed into the room in two easy strides and stood there among us like a visitor from another land, which indeed he was.

He was wearing stiff leather boots and a safari suit, the only clothes he ever wore. His eyes danced with life and his face was tanned almost as black as the tribesmen who followed him on his many expeditions across Africa.

After Papa had kissed each member of the family in turn, he sat in one of the armchairs and scooped me into the air, like a lion with a small cub. He placed me on his knee and, carefully, we sized up one another. It was the first time Papa had taken any notice of me. He had been surprised to learn that he had fathered another child and, though he was disappointed that I wasn't a second son, he told Mama when I was born that I was to be named Afdera, after a live and very masculine volcano he had explored in Abyssinia, or Ethiopia, as it has since become.

I remained on his lap while he talked and joked with the other children. I remember nothing of what he said, although I do recall that he laughed at their uniforms and at my mother's wisdom in acquiring them. Papa was a notorious and outspoken anti-Fascist – and not in private, but openly, the way he lived his life. He was one of the few men who could and did say whatever he wanted without the secret police battering down the door. His knowledge of and intimacy with Africa had its political advantages, especially with the ubiquitous presence of the British. Indeed, Baron Raimondo Franchetti inspired both awe and friendship from Mussolini, not the other way round. My father was a man who knew no fear and wasn't easily impressed.

It was also probably true that behind Papa's smile that day would have been a minefield of hazy uncertainty. He was a man who believed so fervently in freedom that the arrogant, expansionist intrigues that now engaged Europe must have settled over him like an impenetrable cloud. Italy was sending its men and its armour in support of Franco in Spain. Hitler was stirring the pot of national pride and racial hatred. The world was preparing for war.

My father was a man of destiny, and yet he did not belong to these times, as he no longer belonged to his native land. Africa was the home of his heart and he had returned to see his family as if with a premonition that it would be for the last time.

The sky outside was very blue and the drawing-room was speckled in the sunlight that fell through the stained-glass windows. The other children had marched off proudly and the servants had gone about their tasks. Mama was talking and I remained silent on Papa's lap, those moments crystallizing into a memory so vivid it has reached out like a shadow through my life, forever permeating my personal relationships.

Within a matter of days Papa had gone, and a few days later he died in an aeroplane that exploded in mid-air between Cairo and Addis Ababa. A bomb had been planted on board by an *agent provocateur* – probably British, although nobody knows for sure.

Papa's tribe of followers found his body, and his bones remain at rest in his beloved Africa.

I didn't know my father, but I have always missed him.

1 . Salt and Pepper

Life is a jigsaw puzzle and mine, with its mysteries and missing pieces, has been as unplanned as my first meeting with Henry Fonda – the only man I have married, though not the only love of my life.

It was the autumn of 1955 and we were at a dinner party at Piazza Lovatelli, the home of my sister Lorian and her husband, the enormously silly Count Lollo. The setting was perfect – the quaint little *palazzo*, the stars in the clear night sky, the crumbling statues that watched us arrive, their faces frozen in bewilderment. The evening was warm. I was dressed casually and Fonda, who was playing Pierre in the film version of *War and Peace*, arrived with the grave, tormented features that belonged to the character.

Rome was in full season. I had started to see a good deal of Augusto Torlonia, who was still waiting for his divorce from the actress Maria Michi (who became famous in Rossellini's *Rome – Open City*); their marriage had been the subject of much controversy, for, although times were changing, it was still considered disgraceful for the aristocracy to wed outside its ranks. I was shy and frivolous but my family background meant that I was generally considered more suitable as a partner for Augusto – and I was infinitely patient with the long-winded Italian legalities. In spite of all Lorian's complex manoeuvring, I was in no hurry to marry anyone.

When Fonda appeared in our midst my sister was torn between Augusto's bloodline and Fonda's glamour. She worked herself into an intense state of anxiety keeping each under her wing yet a secret from the other.

Fonda was always known to us as Fonda. We never called him Henry; Hank didn't sound melodious with an Italian accent and so, quite simply, he became Fonda.

He had been brought that autumn night to Lorian's dinner party by

I

Audrey Hepburn, the bewitching Natasha in the Carlo Ponti–Dino De Laurentiis film of Tolstoy's masterpiece. It had been three months of constant work and both were a little frayed at the edges – and both were temporarily without their mates: Audrey's husband, Mel Ferrer, was filming with Ingrid Bergman in France; Fonda's wife, Susan, had returned to New York with the children; Augusto was in Milan and I was flirtatiously single among the glittering dark Romans of Lorian's coterie.

When Fonda appeared, I was most impressed. There was something pure and sensitive about him. His eyes were very blue, cool and detached. He looked untouched and untouchable, which I found attractive. We sat down to eat. I was seated a couple of places away from him and, as I couldn't speak or make eyes at him from a distance, I asked him to pass me the salt, then the pepper, the bread, the salad – until in the end he stared at me through the flickering glow of the candles as if to say: who is this creature who keeps asking for things?

At least I had succeeded in capturing his attention, though neither of us then uttered another word.

The evening passed and came to an end and, when I went home, I forgot all about him.

It just so happened that at that same time I had made my first purchase of a pair of paintings, which was quite extraordinary, as nobody I knew then, except married couples, dreamt of doing such a thing.

I had been passing a small picture-framing shop in Via del Babuino, a street famous for its antiques, when I saw the paintings in the window. I don't know anything about paintings, I'm just a great collector of bric-a-brac, but they were so enchanting I decided that I had to have them. In one, there were two nuns playing tennis, which was rather funny and irreligious, and in the other there was a group of monks buying melons from a stall. My favourite colours are rust and dark greens, yet these were bright reds, blue, white and even black, a colour I normally loathe. Nevertheless I wanted them instantly.

I went into the shop, pointed at the paintings and the little man smiled and asked for 100,000 lire (£100) for the pair. I was astonished. 100,000 lire? This was the entire monthly allowance that I received from my family. I tried to charm the man and get him to lower the price, but he said he was reluctant to sell them because an American had bought three similar paintings from him and would probably return for these two.

That made me want to have them even more. I had 20,000 lire in my pocket, which I gave to the man as a deposit and promised to return with the rest the next day, although I didn't have it.

That evening, I was dining with another friend, Annibale Scotti, who used to send me bouquets of flowers and little presents and who had been my admirer since I was sixteen. I told him that I was in love with the paintings and that I simply had to have them.

He looked incredulous: 'Paintings?' he said. 'Paintings?'

'Yes,' I replied. 'Paintings.'

He shook his elephantine head back and forth and then asked: 'What are you going to do with them?'

'It doesn't matter, I'm in love with them,' I said.

He wobbled about like the divine monster he is and I knew he would buy them for me. In truth the money meant little to either of us. He would spend more than that every night on dinner and all I knew about money was that it came as an allowance and it piled up if I didn't touch it – which, of course, seldom happened.

Annibale was a gallant in the most old-fashioned way. He loved young girls like the traditional dirty old man, but he never forced anyone into the bedroom. At our little private dinners I would eat almost nothing and he would devour everything, including me with his eyes. He was podgy and jolly with plump lips that left a damp circle when he kissed my cheeks. He was also my best friend and the most witty and amusing of companions. He called himself the King of the Bidets (he even wore a little golden bidet on a chain around his neck) because his family had made its fortune manufacturing porcelain – including bathrooms. He was a great story-teller and he was always the first person to laugh at himself.

The discussion over the paintings continued through dinner. Annibale grunted and I told him he should do something intellectual for a change, instead of sending me millions of flowers that cost a fortune, and finally, probably to shut me up, he agreed to buy them for me.

We went arm in arm to Via del Babuino the next day and when we entered the shop the man there was most amused. It was a scene straight out of a typical Italian film: the young girl with her sugar-daddy,

3

the appraisal, as if Annibale knew about such things, which of course he didn't, the silent exchange of looks, the intrigue. It was all very silly.

Before Annibale finally parted with his money, I decided to have the paintings reframed with dark blue velvet mounts. At first, the dealer said it would take a week, but I made such a fuss that he agreed to have them ready in two days. For me, everything has to be tomorrow – or it is too late.

With the business settled, we ambled out into the sunshine and went to have lunch.

When I returned to collect the paintings two days later, the man in the shop said the American had been in again. He had decided to buy them himself and was heartbroken that they had already been sold. That made me even more happy with my smiling nuns and melon buyers and I took them home to my flat, a magic little place with a view across the Tiber to the splendid Palazzo della Giustizia.

Life in those days was really rather simple. I was twenty-two, I had lots of admirers and I was overjoyed to be on my own, which was something that set me apart from people of my background. Rich girls just didn't have that freedom – but then, not everyone had my mother. She had become even more eccentric when my father died and each year her idiosyncrasies had become more exotic. She had never taken another lover, which was no doubt the root of the problem. Papa's influence on her had reached out from the grave and lasted throughout her life. He was the powerful one in their relationship and it was he who chose such peculiar names for his four children: Simba, the word for lion in Swahili, my eldest sister; Lorian, my other sister, a year younger, named after the swamp in Ethiopia where the animals go to die; Nanucki – always Nanuck – my brother, whose name came from Papa's journey to the North Pole and who was four years younger than Lorian; and me, Afdera, the baby, six years younger than Nanuck. But more about my family later.

I had collected my paintings, taken them home and had decided to hang them in the small room that led from the spiral staircase to the large boat-shaped terrace, which was to be the scene for several parties in the months ahead.

One of my pleasures was mixing people of different types and backgrounds because I had found that, whatever transpired, the atmosphere would be rather amusing. I had furnished the flat in a sort of extravagant bohemian style with paintings and antiques that seemed to jump out of the walls and off shelves, appearing romantic or Gothic, depending on your mood. Below the stairs I had a *banquette* covered with the odd things I stole each time I visited my mother's house. There was a small drawing-room, two bedrooms and two bathrooms; the second bathroom was absolutely essential as it's the one thing I hate to share. In addition to a few of Mama's bits and pieces, when I moved out, I stole one of her maids and took her with me.

During the weekend that followed my adventure in Via del Babuino, I gave a party and Jean Stein turned up with Mr Fonda. Jean, the girlfriend of writer William Faulkner, was the daughter of Jules Stein, the man who founded the talent agency the Music Corporation of America. She was one of a whole contingent of young Americans who had moved to Rome when it took over from Paris as *the* place to be. Her father and Fonda were friends and she had known him all her life.

I was busy entertaining when they arrived and, although I didn't see Fonda's face when he climbed the spiral stairs and was greeted by the paintings, I learned later that, when he got over his initial shock, he found the coincidence highly comical.

'Isn't life a funny thing,' he would often say – and who am I to disagree with that?

When he appeared on the terrace, I was charming an ambitious but penniless sculptor from Florence and Fonda, now deliciously tantalized, made his way to a dark corner and watched. He was always a man who gravitated to the shadows, a hand in his pocket and his head cocked to one side, as if he was trying to appear shorter than he really was. It's a sad gesture, especially for men who are short – which, of course, Fonda wasn't. He was actually shy, and because of this he would never make the effort to speak to anyone. People would come to him and, if they didn't, he was content with his own company.

Finally, I spotted him and went over to say hello.

'By the way, what lovely paintings you have down there,' he said as soon as the greetings were over. He smiled and then added: 'What are they?'

'Which ones?'

'The nuns playing tennis and . . .'

'Oh, I don't know,' I broke in. 'I saw them and just had to have them.'

'They're very interesting,' he said.

'Are they?' I returned. 'I just thought they were lovely.'

I told him somebody else had wanted them but I got there first and he laughed – and, although he didn't admit that he was the heartbroken American of my story, I guessed and he knew that I'd guessed. And I knew that he knew. It was our first act of complicity.

The arms of the party then pulled us in different directions and, though we didn't speak again, I knew he was now intrigued by the creature who had stolen his paintings.

The third time Henry Fonda and I met was at La Cabala, the elegant and popular night club on Via Monte Brianzo, next to where I lived. It had been hired for the evening by a group of wealthy Romans who were holding a private reception. I have no idea what it was for, not that Italians need a reason. They are always ready to celebrate everything, even their misfortunes.

Lonesome Mr Fonda – every woman in Rome was looking after him – was duly invited, though he apparently only made up his mind to come when he discovered that my sister and I and the others that he knew would be there. Even so he only just made it.

He was working late on *War and Peace* and thirty minutes before midnight he was still in the make-up and costume of a Russian soldier – Pierre, the intellectual, now at the front and tasting the life of the common man. Eventually, the last take was complete and, without changing, Fonda rushed out of the Cinecittà studios and took a taxi to the night club.

I was dancing when he arrived and didn't see the infantryman gazing over the crowd and following my every move. I didn't, but my friends did.

When I sat down, he came to join me.

'Would you like to dance?' he asked. He was very polite and formal.

'Of course,' I answered.

The band began to play 'On the Sunny Side of the Street', which was nice because Hoagy Carmichael, who wrote it, and Fonda had been friends forever. From that night on, in a funny way, it always remained our song.

We danced together very sweetly, with our cheeks touching, in that old-fashioned way, and I was completely charmed. He was inscrutable and mysterious. He didn't talk about himself and he didn't ask me questions about myself either. He said he liked my flat, but he didn't mention the paintings again, not until much later. For my part, I couldn't help thinking that if the paintings hadn't been on the wall when Henry Fonda came to my party, we wouldn't have been dancing cheek to cheek at La Cabala.

When I asked him about *War and Peace*, he said he wasn't happy about the film. He didn't get on well with Dino De Laurentiis and he also thought he was miscast as Pierre.

'It would have been right for Peter Ustinov,' he said. 'I'm no good at all.'

Fonda said he wasn't Pierre, but even at that moment, dressed in the high-buttoned uniform, he had become Pierre. He made the character tall and beautiful.

Fonda was also the perfect match for Audrey Hepburn – off the set, as much as on. They were real friends, a lady and a gentleman – and they could also share their heartaches: Audrey, who was weak, having had a miscarriage earlier that year, was missing Mel Ferrer – and Fonda was wondering where his marriage was going. It was marriage number three and it was clearly going nowhere.

Susan Blanchard had been in Rome with the three children, but had returned to New York when it was time for Jane and Peter to go back to school. Their other child, Amy, was a little dream baby whom they had in fact adopted although she looked like both of them.

At first, Susan and Fonda called each other every day, but the longer the separation lasted the happier they both were to be on their own. Fonda really wanted that marriage to work. His previous wife, Frances Brokaw, the mother of Jane and Peter, had committed suicide, and the two children had accepted and grown fond of Susan. She was a very good stepmother to them.

Mr Fonda had no intention of flirting with me, but he did kiss me very warmly on the cheek that night and we made arrangements to tour the city's art galleries the following day.

For the next two months, Henry Fonda was alone in Rome and everyone was taking care of him. His agent, Arabella Le Maître, now Arabella

Ungaro, adored him and, though they were often together, in the end he started to see more of me than of anyone else.

Our relationship was platonic, but Fonda kept busy with a couple of young starlets in the *dolce vita* set and, when he went off on location with Anita Ekberg, they had a brief affair – unsatisfactory though it turned out.

'I've never met anyone so unsexy in my life,' he told me much later – which was ironic, since Anita was considered the 'sex symbol of the century' at that time.

Annibale, of course, was always hovering on the sidelines. Fonda didn't know that, like Lorian, the King of the Bidets was never a rival but an accomplice – a fellow conspirator whom Henry found confusing.

Fonda had to go away for a while, but when he returned he came to my flat each day to find it flooded with the most gloriously expensive bouquets of flowers.

And that wasn't all that came.

At midday – I never see anyone or like to do anything before midday – a waiter from one of the city's most elegant restaurants would appear at the flat with a glass jar full of blood. I love meat and don't usually want to eat anything but meat, but, strangely, at that time, I was suffering from anaemia. I had become a kind of Dracula. Annibale had decided on the cure and was paying to have the best cuts of beef cooked and drained, and the dark red blood arrived at Via Monte Brianzo with his compliments.

'What is this?' Fonda would say. 'And who keeps sending all the flowers – they must cost a fortune!'

Henry was always mindful of money. When people come up from nothing, they either throw it all away with both hands or they are very careful. Fonda was the careful sort and, although he had a reputation for being mean, with me he never was.

I would listen to his questions and shrug.

'I don't know,' I would reply and then I would sip my macabre medicine, looking wicked *per piacere*, just for the fun of seeing Fonda look shocked.

That, quite naturally, made him like me even more. He thought I was refreshing and amusing and loved nothing more than to have me close at his side as we extended that first trip around the art galleries into an endless tour of the Eternal City. We went from the Colosseum to the

Forum, to the Renaissance palaces of the Campo Marzio quarter, the Vatican, the Arch of Constantine, to Via del Babuino and to the winding, ruined streets of Trastevere, where we hid in discreet *trattorie* and talked about art and architecture and life, all things I knew nothing about – although Henry Fonda did. In spite of his doubts about his performance as Pierre, the reviews when *War and Peace* was released were mainly enthusiastic and, like the character, Fonda was something of an intellectual.

Our secret friendship was slowly becoming more public, although we both remained rather private. We told each other little of what we were doing – and almost nothing of what we were feeling. Even in the future, that was something that would remain submerged. I would misbehave and Fonda would just shake his head and look sombre. He treated me the way he treated the world, with a sort of unsure and uneasy tolerance; he was so guarded, for the first year that I knew him he didn't even shave in front of me. He would get up at half past seven, three hours before I moved my eyelids, wash and then tidy the bathroom so carefully it looked as if no one had been there.

He was a gentleman. He was perfect. He was charming and patient with everyone, even my family, though some members he despised. He was good with waiters and doormen, film crews and servants. The only people he didn't have time for were the handful of spies who had fingered people as Communists during the McCarthy witch hunts, and those people he cut dead. John Wayne was one of them. They worked together, but offstage, Fonda never spoke to the man.

During those early days in Rome we were like two people floating in a bubble. There was never even the mildest suggestion of our having a physical relationship, and that was how it remained when we set off on our first excursion together.

It was marvellous. I was going to Venice, to Treviso, to visit my mother, and Fonda decided to join me with the excuse that he could look up his step-daughter, another Frances, who was studying art, conveniently, in Venice. It was Frances's mother who had killed herself, and when it happened she blamed Henry Fonda. That had passed and now she loved him and hated him at the same time.

We travelled from Rome by train – I never fly if I can avoid it – and it was most romantic having adjoining compartments in the wagons-lits. We shook hands outside our separate doors, just like in an old movie, and when I finally curled up in my blankets it felt strange and exciting to have a famous film star sleeping on the other side of the partition.

Fonda got off the train the next day at the city centre and I went on to Treviso. There a car was waiting to take me to the family home, a run-down Venetian Palladian villa, with a long, winding drive lined by the ruined statues of naked pre-Raphaelite ladies that my brother Nanuck and Ernest Hemingway had once shot up with elephant guns.

I stayed at the house; Fonda booked himself into an hotel. We met each day and went everywhere – twice. It was my city and he saw it through my eyes – the canals, the gondolas, the Bridge of Sighs. We sat under blankets by moonlight, we fed the pigeons, and new feelings began to arise between us. Until then, we had just been good friends, but suddenly, quite suddenly, it was different. We discussed ages for the first time and he said he was two years younger than he was and I said that I was two years older and, in a funny, fateful way, it all added up.

It was then that I decided to show off my American movie star, although that was almost a disaster. Mama was gracious, but vacant. She had no idea who he was. She knew of my apparent engagement to Augusto, although she did not take much interest in that either. She had become Ophelia – quietly mad, and seemed to have got worse since the death of my oldest sister, Simba, who had contracted TB and faded slowly and beautifully. Mama had always been solitary, but then she had become a virtual recluse. The house was full of servants, far too many, though she spoke to no one except her companion, the pauper Baroness Stockhausen, a woman who looked and thought like a Pekinese, and who had been with us since we were all children. She had come when her own family lost its money and, although originally it was to work as a governess, over the years she and Mama had become friends.

Fonda admired the house and looked at the books in the library. There were thousands of them. It was where I hid as a child and read all the novels Mama had said were forbidden: *Lady Chatterley's Lover*, *Ulysses*, Henry Miller's *Tropic of Cancer* and *Tropic of Capricorn*, and a book I read many times, *The Well of Loneliness* by Radclyffe Hall. Everyone in the family was a great reader. Mama loved the French

classics and Simba and Lorian always went to bed with Tolstoy, Dosto-
ievsky or Proust.

When he had finished looking at the books, a car took us to the
station and we set off back to Rome. We were still booked in separate
compartments, but he spent the night in mine.

Fonda's face the following morning, when we got back to my flat,
was bright and guilty; Fidalma the maid didn't say a word – it was all
in her eyes. They were full of wonderful secrets, as if she knew that an
adventure was about to begin – and that she was to be a part of it.

She was right on both counts.

2 . *Good Timing, Bad Timing*

Mr Fonda was sitting secretly on board a Pan Am plane at Rome airport – and I was in the departure lounge surrounded by a great cluster of Italians. It was typical, everyone hugging and crying and shouting out all the things they wanted brought back for them.

It was November 1955, the best month to visit New York, and I was going there for a ten-day holiday so that I could pursue my own thoughts before any big decisions were made. Well, that's what I had told Augusto, who was getting excited because his divorce was approaching and, at the same time, our secret engagement was becoming less of a secret. In spite of this, he didn't produce a ring, except his own wedding ring, which fitted on my thumb, and endless, endless presents. I'm sure he was the first person to think of identity bracelets and he kept giving me these with the swirling letters 'A.A.' and 'A.A.A.'– *Augusto amore Afdera*. They were wonderful. He is now a jewellery designer and that's how it all started.

After I had enough bracelets, he began to give me little medals to hang on them – each one inscribed with something funny that had happened to us. One day we were in Capri and decided to have a picnic, which nobody ever does in Capri. We had spent all day in and out of the sea and in and out of motor boats and then, at about six o'clock, we took our hamper and climbed into the hills to watch the sunset.

It was perfect. Everything was prepared: we had candles, lovely food and the sky was turning orange. Then, suddenly, we were attacked by a great swarm of bees. We ran away and in jest I called Augusto an *assassino*, though when we counted our stings I only found three while he was covered with them. Still, I was furious, and so upset that Augusto decided I deserved my first medal, duly engraved with the legend: 'The bees – Capri'.

So, Augusto marched to the airport with Lorian, with his brother, his cousin. He said goodbye, brought no gifts, but lots of tranquillizers, and off I went with my tourist ticket to join Mr Fonda in the first-class cabin.

The complicity was magic. Going to America was a most exciting thing to do – nobody in my family had ever been. I knew Augusto would be waiting for me in Italy, while here was this strange creature Henry Fonda fussing over me and mysteriously arranging everything. I was feeling marvellous. I didn't have any strong emotional attachments to either. I wasn't in love with Fonda, but there was a special, unique thing between us, all unspoken and unknowing. It was an adventure; I was even a bit scared.

The runway skidded beneath us, Rome became toy town and we climbed high into the clouds. It was an old propeller plane with two beds on board and, naturally, Fonda had reserved them both. I had told him that I had a 'thing' about aeroplanes, so he gave me some Miltown and a glass of champagne – I think my first ever – and between the two I went out like a light. I was put into a berth and the next time I opened my eyes we were about to land in New York.

Fonda had already decided that we were going to get married – not that he had said as much – and had arranged during the coming week to have his favourite sister and brother-in-law come and inspect me. Their names were Jack and Harriet Peacock. She was a big, tall, impressive woman, just like her baby brother, and her husband was someone I liked immediately – and for a funny reason, which I'll come to in due course.

From the airport we went to the Warwick Hotel, a wonderful, old-fashioned place that has since been pulled down and is now the site of the Seagram Building. There was a nice, big room and a bathroom, everything so large, I felt small in them.

Fonda was busy tipping the bell-boy when I walked in to the room to find waiting for me the sweetest thing: a basket of tangerines, my favourite fruit, with a note saying; 'Welcome to New York, My Darling,' which was cosy and nice. No orchids, nothing grand. Fonda never did anything to show off.

The weekend passed with a million phone calls and dinners, and then Fonda came beaming into the room with an announcement: 'You are going to see the most amazing thing of your life,' he told me. 'We are going to the opening night of *My Fair Lady*.'

And it was amazing. It was the most extraordinary night in the history of Broadway. It was like going to the opera in Venice, people were killing each other to get seats. Everyone had booked ages in advance, although Fonda had somehow managed to get tickets the day before. Even then, they had to put extra chairs in the front of the stalls, and that was where we sat.

Now, of course, Rex Harrison and Julie Andrews, the two stars, were both marvellous, but for me what was more marvellous was going out to celebrate after the show with Kay Kendall – Rex's girlfriend and, later, his wife.

I was flabbergasted. She was the most sophisticated, glamorous, amusing, charming, natural, no-bull-shit lady ever. She had a naughty, lovely expression and streams of four-letter words would pour from her mouth like water from a tap, endlessly, words I'd never even heard of – and always with such grace and charm. We were at Sardi's, that institution where the whole world goes to eat after first nights, and everyone's eyes were on our table. Kay was absolutely plastered, but amusing even so.

I was so taken with her that I went immediately to the hairdresser's the next day and had my hair cut in her style. I wanted to be like Kay Kendall – which is something that only happened twice before. Once I wanted to be Vivien Leigh, because she was beautiful, and the other time it was Jennifer Jones, because she was so heroic.

Although I had my hair styled like Kay's, she was really my physical opposite. She had long legs, was very slim with a short waist, a tiny head and a pointed nose. In contrast, I was built like a peasant. But in spite of all that we did have some similarities; we talked the same and, after a while, when I had learned them, I started to use four-letter words – and got drunk too.

After the night at Sardi's we met several times and I grew to like her more and more. She was always 'chippy' and amusing, and angry because she wanted to get married to Rex Harrison and he was keeping her hanging about.

'What's it like for you?' she'd ask. 'You're in the same boat . . .'

I'd shrug and say in all honesty that I wasn't. Kay would snarl and spit out a splendid string of abusive language – and then we would both burst into laughter.

Kay was never quite sure what relationship I did have with Fonda, but then we weren't very sure ourselves. He didn't show his love by what he said, but by what he did. I was embraced by his protection, long before I realized it; he never said anything unpleasant about Augusto Torlonia or anyone else. He never said, 'Well, it's him or me ...' He just let things happen and that's why, when I had to choose, he was the one who won and, I suppose, also the one who lost. Fonda hated failure and our marriage failed, just like his first three.

New York, New York. It was a magic time. Officially, I was supposed to stay for ten days. It turned out to be three weeks, and they went by like a minute. The phone rang so much, it was hot just to touch – and, as often as not, the calls were long distance from Rome. One of Augusto's cousins was working in the film industry in New York and, as the movie world is about as big as a thumbnail, he knew that I was seeing Fonda – and had whispered as much in Augusto's ear.

Augusto didn't believe a word of it. He knew I had lots of admirers, and that was what he told his cousin. I didn't need to be warned; it was obvious from Augusto's conversation and 'innocent' questions that little rumours had wandered back to Italy. He never actually came right out and demanded to know what was going on – he was too weak, or too nice – although, finally, he did go to my sister and ask her if there was any fire under the smoke. Lorian, who had then taken the role of my mother, everyone's mother, said yes, I was seeing Henry Fonda – but that there was nothing serious between us.

'Let her be; let her be,' she told him; and that's what she told everybody.

And everybody listened – except Annibale Scotti.

He thought it was marvellous that I was in New York, away from my family, away from everyone – not that he telephoned, that wasn't his style. He turned up in person.

So now, on the lovely, crisp November days while Mr Fonda was preparing *Twelve Angry Men* – the most important project of his life, the only film he ever produced and one that won lots of awards and didn't earn a penny – there was the King of the Bidets to take me out shopping and buy me lots of presents. Gucci was the very minimum a girl would accept in those days. The little gifts mounted up and, whereas I'd left home with only one suitcase, I returned with five. I also had a mink coat – and that did cause a few problems ...

Annibale was wonderful company in Rome, and in New York he was even better. Everyone was so amused by him; his English was deplorable. He was always overdoing it: over-gushing, over-gauche, over-charming and over-funny – which saved him.

He was light relief – and that was exactly what I needed. Fonda's friends were all establishment people, whom I found could be hard work, and there was another small complication: I had met a man who quite took my breath away.

Nothing had been planned – least of all complications – but almost as soon as I arrived in New York I met Renaldo and Mimi Herrera, some Venezuelan friends I had made when we were on a cruise together two years earlier. That had been the most famous and talked-about gathering of all time, a celebration that wasn't celebrating anything, made marvellous by Elsa Maxwell, the queen of the party hostesses. She had been given a few million spare drachmas by Onassis, with the idea of putting Greece on the map – Greece was the poor man of Europe: lots of history, but about as much *beau monde* as the jungle. So five hundred people from all over the world were invited – the fast set, the jet set, New York's high society – all well-known couples and just a few single girls: me, Marina Cicogna, Frances, who's now the Duchess of Rutland, and another one or two I can't remember.

It was amazing, special, unforgettable – a dream. Everyone became great friends. Two years passed and, when I went off to have dinner with the Herreras, I met their son, Renaldito, a man who was very attractive and, really, the best news of all. (The Herreras had a home in New York and were one of the wealthy old families who had lived for generations in Caracas.)

I knew lots of people in New York and fitting them all into my diary was a nightmare, but an amusing one. I kept Mr Fonda a secret as much as I could and, when I had an engagement in the evening, I would have to make excuses so that I could rush off and meet him when he had finished rehearsals, or whatever he had been doing. We would have dinner or go to a club and then spend the night at his home, a brownstone house on East Seventy-fourth Street. Then, the next morning, when Fonda went off to work again, I would rush back to the Warwick, ready to start a fresh round of appointments. I was like Holly Golightly, always travelling so fast that nothing was left behind but the faint trace of perfume.

It was a whole new world, a world of real excitement. Fonda was why I went to America, but once I was there I didn't intend to miss a thing. Annibale took me shopping, Renaldito wooed me, Fonda spoiled me – and there were others, nobody knowing why I was always in such a rush, no one knowing what to think, or what to expect. I kept each segment of the day separate, like orange pieces on a plate. I became a master at manipulating time, but then I became so confident I became careless. There was some overlapping of appointments and finally, the *dénouement*.

It was a perfectly normal lunchtime. I had spent the morning in bed writing to Mama, eventually dressed and then set off downstairs to my appointment at the hotel bar. I walked in with a radiant smile – and almost fell through the floor. Standing in a row, slightly apart, and each suddenly glancing from me to the other three, were Henry Fonda, Annibale Scotti, Renaldito Herrera and the producer Michael Mindley.

'Oh, my God!' I said.

'How wonderful, I was just passing, what a coincidence,' said Renaldito, instinctively Latin and naughty and knowing how to say the right thing.

Annibale, of course, was the opposite.

'I'm here,' he said. 'I came ...' – the English language sounding all sandy on his tongue.

Fonda looked from face to face and then stared at me. 'I thought I'd come and ...' He didn't finish his sentence.

Michael – I'd met him when he was doing *Porgy and Bess* with Lennie Bernstein – was a cheeky Peter Pan who took his lead from Renaldito. 'Why, hello,' he said. 'Who are you all? How nice to meet you.'

Annibale's bottom lip, always drooping, drooped even more, Fonda's eyes were like saucers, and I was livid. I had been so good at timing, I mean *timing* – and then they all go and turn up together.

There was only one thing for me to do: I turned on my heels and walked straight out of the door.

Outside, it was a lovely, bright day and I crossed the road and went into Central Park. Fonda and I had a weakness for going there and riding in the little horse-drawn carriages – it was safe in those days – and as my heels crunched over the frosty grass, I completely forgot that

I was supposed to be in a bad mood. I wandered out of the park and along Park Avenue. I looked at the trees, all spindly with handfuls of snow, and I remembered the story Fonda had told me on one of our midnight excursions. He said the trees had been planted in memory of all the soldiers who had died in the last war and below each one was a different name. I thought it was a charming idea and now, as I read the names, it was Fonda I thought of.

My first reaction at the Warwick was to decide never to speak to any of those men again, but I was glad when Fonda called that afternoon. I offered no explanation for the 'coincidence' and he didn't mention it until we went out to eat that night. He had been awfully quiet and then his smooth brow was suddenly covered in lines.

'Who were those men today?' he asked. 'It was a ... a bit of a surprise.'

'I don't know,' I replied. 'Just admirers.'

Fonda shook his head and I got on with my food. (It was Chinese, another new discovery and something that was unheard of in Rome. Eating exotic food was an adventure and we dined happily on Japanese food the next night, and Indian the night after, although that was too hot and I didn't like it at all.)

From the restaurant, we went back to Seventy-fourth Street, where I wandered restlessly from room to room, wondering what changes I would make if it was my house. It was very conservative – and practically empty. Fonda's divorce from Susan Blanchard was nearly through and she had taken half the furniture, half the pictures, half of everything. The big four-poster bed where they had slept was still there, but that didn't worry me, and I remember finding a lipstick and a pair of jeans. I'm not a blue jeans person and never was. On the contrary, I was very formal. Whatever style was 'in' – I was in something else. One thing Susan couldn't take with her were her colours – pinks, reds and whites. It was charming, no ghosts. It was like she had never passed through.

I looked thoughtful and Fonda must have imagined that I felt uneasy in another woman's house. He then told me that his brother-in-law, Jack Peacock, was a very good decorator – in Nebraska – and that he was going to redo the place 'from top to bottom'.

'Wonderful,' I said.

He grinned and looked happy and didn't know then that, six months after the redoing, I'd move permanently to New York – and it would all have to be redone again.

The famous dinner with the Peacocks took place the following weekend. We met at the '21' – the only place to go – a terrible mistake, as all the film people congregate there, including, at the time, Ascanio Branca and all those who had now started to see me with Fonda and wonder who I was.

So there I sat, Harriet quietly watching and Jack Peacock like a cartoon of an Englishman at his club with rosy red cheeks and a moustache. He could have been Colonel Blimp, only older – solid, middle-aged, middle class, from the middle of America. I thought they were both adorable – especially him.

'Ah!' he exclaimed. 'Afdera. Hank talks about you all the time and he never usually talks about anyone.'

Hank laughed and Harriet laughed and I smiled and there was a little silence before Jack Peacock leaned across the table and said with even greater enthusiasm: 'Afdera, you have the most beautiful teeth. I've never seen such attractive teeth.'

Teeth!

I've no idea why he thought about my teeth. I mean, people have been known to say nice things about my eyes – and other things: 'filled with the secrets that go back to Eve', according to Howard Teichmann, the author of Fonda's biography – but *teeth*? I thought it was charming and it made me love Jack immediately.

Now Harriet was far more cautious. Like Jack, she also seemed very English, only a County lady, straight-backed, reserved, saying almost nothing and following my every move. She did realize that, if nothing else, I did make Fonda happy – and young – and that was important while the loose ends of his marriage were tucked carefully into place. She had spent the afternoon with Susan Blanchard, who had told Harriet that Fonda had made her miserable: he was stingy and tough and cold, and she was going to be just as tough when it came to the divorce settlement.

All that must have been like powdered glass in poor Harriet's bloodstream. To her, Fonda was God and now, even if she didn't want to like me she had to like me – and, little by little, she found no reason not to. A bit later she told her brother that she found me 'completely natural' – she wasn't talking about teeth – and, though I'm not sure why her opinion was so crucial, it was, and somehow I passed the test.

As for Susan Blanchard, like the rest of the universe she now knew that I was on the scene and this had upset her. She didn't want to be married to Fonda any more but, like most married women when the marriage was over, she didn't want her partner to find someone else too quickly. She had lots of lovers herself, but there wasn't a steady one.

There were endless intrigues and undercurrents – not that I was *that* interested. Jack Peacock's cheeks grew redder as he shuffled back the champagne and talked about interior decorating. Harriet watched me: Fonda watched Harriet watching me and, since I was 'completely natural', the dinner party was remembered as a great success.

Another week had passed and, with it, all its wonderful complications. I was getting closer to Fonda, without really knowing it or admitting it to myself, and it was no doubt because of this that our first minor disagreement resulted in my telling him that I wasn't going to see him for a couple of days.

'It's nothing dramatic,' I said. 'I just want to be on my own for a while, and Renaldito wants to take me to the theatre.'

'Fine, fine, what a great idea,' he broke in. 'You should see your friends.'

His eyes were bright blue like a summer sky and I knew he was up to something. He was a chess player, always making the most mischievous moves.

We left it at that. Renaldito came to pick me up at the Warwick the following night and off we went in a limousine to watch the play – late, and crept through the darkness to find our seats. The performance was breathtaking and fantastic, although I cannot remember what we saw – clap, clap, clap, the curtain came down and whom did I see wandering up the aisle next to me when we left?

Fonda!

And on his arm was his daughter Jane, pretty and plump in a grey plaid suit and a grey sweater – the real college girl from Vassar – not knowing who I was, although I knew her from the photographs at the house. Fonda turned his head sideways and gave me his funny look and neither of us said a word.

Outside, the limousine pulled up for Renaldito and me – and Fonda, who was right behind us, had to whistle for a taxi. Luckily, he was an expert whistler and could stop taxis when they were miles away.

I sat back with my handsome Venezuelan. The snow was falling, all glittery like stars in the Broadway lights; the streets were full of people and cars – and I felt peculiarly unbalanced. What was Fonda doing at the theatre? And what was Jane doing with him? She had to come into the city by train and it took hours. She couldn't have come just to see that play. It was a mystery. Fonda never told you what he was doing. He just set everything up and watched what happened.

Our limousine came to a halt at the El Morocco, a dark and smoky night club that was filling up with Europeans, and from there, before the evening was through, I called Fonda. I couldn't go back to the house and sleep because Jane was there – Jane was very fond of Susan – but for the first time I wanted to more than anything else. For so long we had been playing cat and mouse, an endless chess game, and it was a major move to bring out his daughter, the Queen.

'Are you free for lunch tomorrow?' Fonda asked. He sounded like a choir boy.

'Yes,' I replied, 'Of course I am.'

'At the bar. . . in the Warwick?' he said. 'About one.'

'I'll be there.'

If nothing else, I was always punctual – nearly always.

It's a funny thing, but it was from that moment, not in Rome and not in Venice, but from that very second that something between us clicked.

Not long after, two amusing episodes occurred, one in New York and one in California.

The first was at Romanoff's, a restaurant where the 'wives' go to be seen and to talk to Mike Romanoff, a charming, make-believe prince. He had come to join the lunch-time table I was sharing with Lauren Bacall. Betty, as she is better known away from the film fans, has been in and out of my life forever, sometimes an enemy, more often a friend, always loud and cheerful, with wicked dark eyes and arms that she throws about like an Italian. Everyone was witty and amusing, when who should walk in but a little, solid man smoking a cigar the size of a chimney – a man I didn't recognize, who came straight up and shot out his hand, first to Betty, and then to me.

I was just about to shake it, when someone said he was the producer Darryl Zanuck, and I pulled my hand away as if I was about to touch fire.

'I just remembered, I'm not supposed to,' I said.

There was a silence. Betty's dark eyes flashed – she loved it. Then the man slowly took his cigar out of his mouth.

'Fonda?' he said.

I nodded.

'He's a shit.'

'That's okay,' I shrugged. 'He thinks the same about you.'

Darryl Zanuck plugged his cigar back into his lips and, as he puffed out a great cloud of smoke, someone laughed and everyone joined in. It was funny; no one was embarrassed – though I didn't tell Fonda what had happened.

Zanuck, who was one of the most important men in movies, John Wayne, the tallest, and the actor Myron McCormick, who had shared a room with Fonda and had been with him in the University Players during the Depression, were three people Fonda had cut out of his life – and I was barred from even so much as shaking their hands.

Late one night we were in a basement jazz club, a real hole in the wall where the New York intelligentsia went to swoon over the latest in the musical avant-garde. Dave Brubeck was playing, Fonda was drumming his fingers on the table in ecstasy and I had ordered a plate of spare ribs just to stay awake.

'It's an acquired taste,' Fonda whispered (the jazz, not the spare ribs). Though I did learn to like the music and now often go to Ronnie Scott's club in London, then it was a sleeping pill to me. I sat there, so bored to tears it was a relief when the food arrived, and then the whole tray full of food came crashing to the table.

Someone took a photograph, Fonda broke into fits of laughter, I looked round and, standing there in a white jacket, just like a waiter, was the director John Huston. He had seen Fonda, which made him turn and tilt the tray – and then he saw me, which made him drop it.

'What are you doing with *this* one?' he asked Fonda. 'And what are *you* doing with *him*?' he enquired of me.

I shrugged, Fonda continued laughing and Dave Brubeck shook his head as if to say, 'Philistines!'

I had first met John at the Venice Film Festival. He thought I was an attractive, up-and-coming young thing, which I suppose I was. He sometimes stayed with the family in Treviso and for a while I had a little crush on him. He was evil and fascinating, dramatic. He had tiny monkey eyes and a slow, slow voice that hypnotized you. He was very successful with women. If he focused on a lady, it was rare for her not to fall under his spell. But I was always wary. I knew he was like a snake or Rasputin: once under his spell he could destroy you. He was also enormously talented, a multi-dimensional man, with an extra twinkle, an extra vision that made him one of those special directors whose films were always something quite extraordinary.

He could have been a European, French or Russian. He was also a snob – and that was why he bought a castle in Ireland, became a gentleman and a Master of Fox Hounds. He was beautiful in hunting pink – he had long arms and legs and actually looked better on a horse than on the ground.

Years later, in 1961, I went to stay with Huston for Christmas and we made up a foursome with John Steinbeck and his extremely nice American wife – a lady who was forever telling her husband what to do. John would do whatever she said, for he was a nice, easy-going ex-drunkard. He was Fonda's best man at one of his weddings and, of course, he wrote *The Grapes of Wrath*, Fonda's first big success in films. Like all clever people, John Steinbeck had that very slow way of talking about interesting, fascinating things – not that I listened with any great concentration. At the time, I was so confused, my mind was always somewhere else.

A lot of years had gone under the bridge by then. I was separated from Fonda. John Huston and I had a long-standing, if uneasy, attraction and I thought, well, why not: let's take the plunge!

The setting was ideal: a fairy castle in the middle of rolling green hills and woodlands, the clean rain and, below ground in the cellars, the most amazing Japanese garden, big plants, a sauna, a swimming-pool where everyone swam naked. It was all very erotic. John had decided that, finally, this was the time but, when it came to it, I couldn't. It was impossible. I felt a mental chemistry, but not a physical one. Everything about John was too long: his arms, his legs, his prehistoric monkey face – everything! It was most embarrassing – in fact, I had to tell him a little lie – that I had a strange illness. He didn't believe me, but he had to pretend to.

It could and it should have been a magic Christmas, but it wasn't. There were Huston and Steinbeck, both famous, talented men, but I had just broken up with somebody I loved, perhaps the only man I ever loved, about whom I will write later.

3 . Indecision

It was Christmas 1955 and I was back in Rome with my new mink coat, something young girls simply didn't wear in those days. I stepped straight off the plane and into an unhappy atmosphere generated by Augusto and his family. My long-suffering fiancé didn't actually say anything, he just looked sorry for himself and gave me lots of presents, which irritated me. It took some time, but he did eventually pluck up the courage to ask about the coat. Fonda had bought it in a rare wave of generosity, but I said it was a gift from one of the nice ladies that I had first met on that famous Greek cruise and then met again in New York.

'It's her old coat,' I explained. 'It looked so well on me, she said I could have it.'

Augusto should have made a scene, but instead, his chin dropped on to his chest.

'Let her be, let her be,' Lorian told him again – and that was that. She was playing out her sisterly role, so that she could poke her nose into everything. Mama was by now having electric shock therapy; Nanuck was just, well, Nanuck, and my only other connection with childhood was Baroness Stockhausen, not that anyone had asked her advice about anything since the day she was born.

Ever since my childhood, Lorian and I had had a strange relationship, and in the end she disappointed me for many reasons. She had an extraordinary way of destroying people – with compliments, with praise always lightly dipped in acid. 'What a wonderful, amusing, handsome man,' she would say, looking sad as she leaned over to whisper: 'It's such a shame about the B.O.' Or: 'What a lovely girl Afdera is – what a pity she's a nymphomaniac' – as if I wasn't her sister; or, perhaps, because I *was* her sister.

She was master of the wicked word, but instead of putting people off, everyone was attracted to her – moths to the flame – and even her husband was always faithful, though in his younger days Loffredo Gaetani Lovatelli had been a famous philanderer. He was a war hero, fighting with the Italian Fascists who went to help Franco in Spain, and it was there that he suffered the most terrible wound – one of his *cojones* was shot off. Undeterred – and no doubt wondering about his manhood – he fathered two children in Spain and returned to have an *amour* with the daughter of a prominent political figure. Then he had six more children with my sister.

In spite of everything, Lorian and Lollo were my guardian angels, the same as Annibale, who was always there and always refreshing. He pursued hundreds of women but he still pursued me because he had never caught me. It was what I needed to take my mind off the *big* decision – Augusto, with his kindness, or Fonda, who offered the world in his silences and funny smiles.

How many girls have such problems? I suppose I was lucky; not that I thought so at the time. I found it impossible to choose, I hated the pressure – I wasn't so sure that I wanted to tie myself down with anyone. Strangely enough, although the exact opposite was in Arabella Ungaro's mind, in a funny way she helped to add the few extra grains of sand that eventually tilted the balance.

Fonda had made a fleeting trip back to Rome to do some studio work on *War and Peace* and just after he left I got a call from Arabella, who said she 'wanted to have a word with me'. She was Fonda's agent, but she was more than that, she was very protective and also had a crush on him herself. She was a close friend of Lorian and, in a way, from a different generation.

In my bedroom I had a life-size portrait photograph of Fonda that had been taken for *Twelve Angry Men* – he had a strange expression as if he was saying: 'To Marry or Not To Marry?' That was what I said whenever I found myself peering into his blue eyes.

So, Arabella arrived. The maid showed her into the bedroom – I was sitting up in bed having breakfast – and she stared straight at the photograph.

'That is who I want to talk to you about,' she said.

I smiled.

'I hear things are becoming serious between you?'

'Yes,' I replied, 'they are becoming very serious.'

She took a deep breath and blurted out: 'Don't hurry him – he's a very special man – he's had a lot of tragedies in his life.'

I was silent.

'You are very immature – you're full of charm – he's falling in love with you, but you can only hurt him.'

'I can only hurt him?'

'Yes, yes, can't you see, you're not ready yet?'

I had been patient for long enough.

'Now you listen to me,' I said. 'It's none of your business.'

Arabella turned bright red, looked daggers at me and marched out of the room.

The door closed and I looked at Henry Fonda: 'To Marry or Not To Marry?' I was closer to making a decision.

Arabella's sudden visit had come after Fonda's last trip to Rome, when a photographer caught him emerging from my flat on Via Monte Brianzo and splashed the photograph and question across the gossip columns: 'What was Henry Fonda doing outside this apartment building at eight in the morning?' Naturally, I denied everything and, though at the time I couldn't imagine what the *paparazzo* was doing there at such an unholy hour, I have since wondered if Fonda's publicists may have set the whole thing up. No publicity is bad publicity.

Fonda had gone again, back to the nervous strain of *Twelve Angry Men* – it was driving him crazy – and maintaining our love affair by post. A letter or a telegram came every day and Fidalma brought it to me with breakfast. Some days there wasn't a letter and she would look distraught, but then, the next day there would be two and she would be all smiles again. Fonda, in his quiet, unassuming way and without saying a word, had completely seduced her.

The year came to an end. It snowed in Rome, as it had snowed in New York, and it was a relief when the leaves began to bud on the trees. The Tiber stopped looking sorry for itself and Fonda and I started our series of 'secret' holidays.

The first place we went to was Jerusalem, where he had been made the 'Man of the Year'. I've no idea why, and I hated it. Hours on the plane, speeches I didn't go to and then back again with a suitcase full of photographs. There were a couple of trips to America. When Fonda's film *Twelve Angry Men* eventually opened at the Capitol Theatre in

Manhattan, it was taken off after only one week. It was a dismal failure and Fonda felt suicidal.

'That was the first picture I've ever produced,' he said. 'And it's going to be the last one.'

He was worried that his career would be ruined, but it wasn't. In fact, even though the film was withdrawn in the United States, in Europe it was a tremendous success. It won a number of prizes, including first prize at the Berlin Film Festival and another prize in Italy.

That was to come and meanwhile I enjoyed the days as they grew warmer and the preparations we were now making for a cultural tour of Spain. Toledo, to see where El Greco painted; Madrid, to visit the Prado; Logroño and Seville, where we saw the great matador Antonio Ordóñez perform at the *corridas*. It was his big season: he killed sixty-six bulls and was gored three times, once very badly. It was my début. The sun was hazy through the dust. There were tiers of people shouting and sweating. The bull was charging and making terrible noises, and the bullfighter, tall and motionless, all silver and glinting like a razor blade, twirled the red cape. His sword plunged into the poor beast – *olé*, *olé* – the Spaniards all surged forward, and there we were standing next to Ernest and Mary Hemingway.

Papa's mouth dropped open. The last thing in the world he imagined was seeing me there with a man like Fonda. Not that he actually recognized him straight away, and not that Fonda recognized Hemingway, which wasn't so surprising. Hemingway was at his worst: he had a long beard and his skin was crumbling off like bits of cake. He was also fat, like a cuddly Teddy bear. To me, it was very funny. We all squinted at each other in the sunlight and then, when everyone had kissed and shaken hands, Papa looked at me as if to say: How do you know Fonda? – and Fonda looked at me as if to say: How do you know Hemingway?

It was one of those long stories and went way back to my father. Hemingway, of course, was an Africanologist and my father was a hunter as well as an explorer. Hemingway's safaris were years after my father's death, but his exploits had lived on. In fact, he was one of Hemingway's heroes and with good reason: it was said that my father didn't have to go to the animals, for they came to him. The lion would come up and lick his hand: if there was a python, it would just look at him and python away. It was difficult for Papa (my Papa) to kill the animals, and he did so only by shooting them from a great distance, and then only so that he could bring them home and furnish his own private museum. It occupied one of the wings in our house in Treviso. It was a haunted, frightening place that I didn't like at all – the animals all stuffed and mounted in attacking positions: the lioness eating a zebra, a python killing a gazelle. There was chintzy material on the walls, show cases and vast, grotesque heads with glass eyes that followed you everywhere. When the family sold the house – it was the one where all the statues had been shot up – my brother gave the animal museum to the Treviso city council.

Nanuck had first met Hemingway by chance in Venice, probably at Harry's Bar, and immediately they became friends. Hemingway was surprised to meet the son of the great Baron Franchetti, and Nanuck, who had never really had a father, was pleased to suddenly have this father figure to look up to. They were similar in some ways, they liked the *macho* in each other, the mad streak. When Hemingway was sick, he would still go out fishing and hunting, and Nanuck was the same. He had been told not to shoot because it was making him deaf, but he kept on shooting, finally went deaf – and still kept on.

Hemingway came to Venice in the winter, when I was fifteen, and as each year went by, he became more attached to the city and the people – the ordinary people, the boatmen and waiters and chefs. He was a bar person, going from place to place and talking for hours and inventing drinks with the barmen. He spoke awful Italian and learned all the Venetian gutter slang, the only words he did remember when the drink had driven everything else from his mind.

When Nanuck brought him out to the house, we all lined up formally to shake the great writer's hand – he was nice and casual and interested in everything and seemed to like us all.

As we came to know Hemingway, he stopped liking us merely as a family and grew to like us as individuals; Mama because she was eccentric and loved the country; Lorian because she was beautiful; Nanuck because everyone loves Nanuck; and Simba for reasons that were more deep, more abstract. Hemingway was extremely perceptive, and in Simba he seemed to see something unique. She had an aura about her, like a saint. She didn't know how to flirt with a man, but was a nurse and had every possible degree in nursing you can get in Italy. Hemingway first came a few years after the war had ended and by then Simba had already contracted TB. She was also suffering from anorexia and had been for a long time; she didn't eat a thing; she had a tiny, slender body and a long, swan neck, soft features and brown hair. She looked a bit like Dorothy McGuire, an actress I always liked, probably because she looked like my sister. Simba was thirty-three when she died – the same age as Jesus Christ.

Hemingway's feelings for me changed with the years. At first I was just a child in the shadow of my sisters, but then a year came when he gave me a saucy look and said: 'Afdera, you have the most marvellous tits,' and tweaked one. I screamed and was most offended and also a little flattered. He was there for the duck shooting. In the past, I had never gone – it meant getting up at five in the morning, and the only way I could do that was by not going to bed. That's what we all did: we sat up drinking *grappa* – it only needed one glass to kill me – and, when we set off, the moon was still slipping through the darkness.

We were going to Nanuck's shooting preserve in San Gaetano, near Portogruaro, a journey of an hour in old, flat-bottomed boats through giant trees that made an archway over the river. The mist rolled before us in curling blue waves and the icy cold clawed under my coat and clothes like tiny hands. When we finally arrived at our destination, the boatmen set out wooden decoys, while the hunters broke open the heavy cartridge cases and hid themselves in large, half-sunken barrels.

When the sun came up, I could see the white tips of the distant mountains, the snow in the trees dropped and thudded to the ground and, when the ducks moved above, the guns roared out and the birds fell gracelessly into the river. The dogs, which had been shivering earlier, became excited as they panted back and forth. They gripped the green heads of the ducks in their teeth with great care so as not to damage the plump, rounded bodies.

The noise and the blood were potent stimulants. Nanuck and Papa and the other men grinned and let out streams of white breath. The heat of the moment warmed me and put me in touch with something barbaric and primeval – the hot blood of my ancestors, my father. New feelings, things I didn't completely understand were pricking the surface. I caught Papa's eyes on me. I must have blushed and he laughed his vast belly laugh. He was so filled with life, he instilled pleasure in the people around him: Nanuck, me, the boatmen now lining up the ducks, breast up, along the side of the boats. The sun had become warmer and was moving across a sky that was solid blue without a speck of cloud.

We returned to the house, food was cooked and we warmed ourselves in front of a blazing fire of beech logs. Papa was at his happiest, drinking the wine and going over everything that had happened on the shoot. He loved all the small things that others didn't see, details he described so minutely that gave his work that extra dimension. The windows slowly darkened. The wind was roaring through the trees outside, the men were boasting and filling the room with their stories. We had been up all the previous night and now, as the others yawned and crept off to bed, I stayed up late into that night with Papa talking, the hours blurring and becoming dream-like. All that we did and said merges into a memory that words cannot capture. What do people talk about when darkness falls and they are left alone? I remember only the feelings, new feelings that had awakened. I had entered a new world that was, in some ways, to shape the future.

The next day, Mary returned from her sight-seeing tour. The season ended and Papa left. The following year we were all a year older. Papa had by then become a friend of the Ivancich family, which included Gianfranco, who was a close friend of Nanuck, and his younger sister Adriana, a beautiful and talented artist who stuck to Papa like glue.

A year or so later, when Hemingway's book *Across the River and Into the Trees* was in the shops, the Italian press made a big thing of the character Renata and published photographs of Adriana and me with a big question mark hanging over the identity of the writer's mystery liaison. It was silly and funny, and it did no harm to my 'image'! I was in my Vivien Leigh period and was travelling around Italy as the *ingénue* in a theatre company. I was going to be a famous actress and I revelled in the publicity, even though I knew that the Contessa Renata was only a figment of Hemingway's vivid imagination. He may have taken my eyes and way of talking and combined them with Adriana's hair and olive skin, but Renata was a mixture of all the young girls Papa knew or wanted – or thought he wanted.

The problem was that Adriana Ivancich took it all far too seriously. She started to write to Papa and, naturally, he wrote back. He was a letter person, as everyone these days is a telephone person. He sent letters to waiters and barmen, but that didn't mean he was in love with them. Hemingway imagined that he defended Venice in the war, which he didn't – he was a romantic, and that was what Adriana fell for, until finally she became so obsessed with the imaginary relationship that it put the seed of madness into her mind and caused endless disasters in her life.

In spite of the undying love she had for Hemingway, she married twice, the first time to a Greek by the name of Mona – a crude Venetian term for the secret part of the female anatomy. So, for a while, she was known as Mrs C——, which was so bad she had to leave Venice. She eventually divorced the Greek, and married a Mr Rex. When that marriage went wrong, she started to grow attached to the past – and that's when the real obsession began. What really happened between Hemingway and Adriana no one knows – they probably just did a bit of necking on a gondola, and Papa did that with everyone.

The story took a new twist when Adriana turned up in London and put all Hemingway's letters up for auction at Christie's. They sold for about £50. It shocked me; it was a strange thing to do after such great love. Finally, she wrote a book about her romance with the writer – it was after Papa had died – and when that was a flop, she committed suicide.

My own friendship with Ernest Hemingway continued in a more formal way. I saw him when our paths happened to cross in Venice, although I did make a point of visiting him some time later, in the spring of 1954, when he was staying in a small cabin on the outskirts of the ski resort of Cortina. All his old diseases had returned and he was still recuperating after his plane crash in Uganda: the lightweight Cessna had gone out of control in avoiding a flock of ibex and then dived into the African bush. Hemingway was with Mary and the pilot and all three were saved by being picked up the next day by a Nile cruiser, the *Murchison*, the very boat that had been rented by John Huston during the making of *The African Queen*. By then, the whole world had read Hemingway's obituary in the newspapers – but Papa didn't die so easily.

We talked about this and about Hemingway – '*io, io, io,*' like all writers he talked mostly about himself – and I was just amazed at how dreadful he looked. He was red and fat, with an eye-shade, tiny round glasses and tiny haunted eyes that never blinked. He was really quite a pathetic figure at this time, but somehow I still knew that inside there was this brain ticking away and taking everything in. I was surprised by him but I think he was just as surprised by me. I had gone through a lot of changes. I was no longer a teenager, but a grown woman. I was twenty-one. I had become charming and frivolous. Papa didn't think I was particularly intelligent, but he considered me 'intuitive' and, on that basis, there was always plenty for us to talk about.

Hemingway was a man who loved having visitors; he was curious about everyone, even though his wife did all she could to chase them away. I couldn't stand Mary. She was a pain. She was always there. She was jealous of anybody who was younger than she was. She was awful; she had piercing, pinhead eyes, her face was covered in lines and she thought every woman in creation was after her husband.

I certainly wasn't. The last trip I made to the Hemingways' was by sledge with Annibale Scotti, then a new and most amusing companion. My little world was growing bigger.

So, there we are, two years later, standing in a sea of Spaniards in Seville, the sky darkened by flying hats, Hemingway and Fonda looking at each other and Mary with her beady, close-together eyes evaluating me carefully. Papa was just as amazed, but by then, I'm afraid to say, he was more 'there' than 'here'. Ten years earlier, he would have turned to Fonda, patted him on the back and cracked a joke.

We went to a bar for drinks and Papa talked about Ordóñez – he was in love with him and followed him everywhere. Fonda seemed a little glazed and Mary just stared at my clothes. I was wearing a dark blue dress, white gloves, a pin and pearls, all very proper, but hardly the right thing for the *corrida*. I never followed the rules.

That was the last time I saw Hemingway. Five years later, of course, he killed himself with a double-barrelled shotgun; it was June 1961 – and my own life was at a very peculiar stage.

I don't know if Fonda fell in love with bull-fighting that day, but on our honeymoon we went back to Spain, to Pamplona, to see the bulls running through the streets. Like all introverted men, there was a part of Fonda that was excited by brutal things. He was also an artist, an oil painter, and the violence appealed to the opposite side of his nature. He was a man of many facets and it took a long time before he revealed them all, if indeed he ever did.

Just before dawn during our first night in the ancient medieval city, while we were lying there awake, the most extraordinary thing happened. In the silence, we suddenly heard the sound of wooden flutes in the darkness outside. We hurried across the room and, as we looked out of our window, five young men in berets were passing. They were Basques, tall and thin, with pure faces, like monks. Fonda had actually noticed them during the afternoon. While I and everyone else were caught up in the drama of the bull run, he was seeing something outside it all, something that didn't belong to the noise and the blood.

The sad, beautiful sound faded and once more the street was empty. The musicians vanished and the silence resettled, thick and heavy, like a fall of snow. The music had gone, but something remained. The moment was special, as if Fonda had made it happen; it was our moment and from it there was a lesson to be learned.

From the first time I stepped on board an aeroplane to fly from Venice to London, where I went at fourteen to take an English course, I have hated flying. Someone once gave me Erica Jong's book *Fear of Flying*, thinking it would help, although help what, I'm not too sure. It's a very naughty book! My own fear became obsessive and it all began that year, in 1956. It was before aeroplanes were jet propelled, and in twelve months I must have circled the earth I don't know how many times – Israel, Spain, New York and then back and forth to Los Angeles.

In Los Angeles I was the guest of Jack and Peggy Bolton, who were Fonda's accomplices in our so-called secret affair, as Annibale Scotti and some of my girlfriends in Treviso and Cortina were mine. It was so exciting. I arrived at the Beverly Hills Hotel, checked in as 'Miss Smith' and went off to my suite to find the most enormous bed I had ever seen. It was Hollywood, so I thought it was all perfectly normal. What I didn't know, and what I didn't find out for ages, was that in those days the rooms only came with twin beds. But twins were obviously not big enough for Henry Fonda, who had instructed Jack Bolton to have them moved out and the monster bed moved in. The room also had an ice-box complete with instant espresso and all sorts of Italian things, which I also thought was normal, but it wasn't. Fonda had arranged it all as secretly he arranged everything.

Fonda was busy making an Alfred Hitchcock film, *The Wrong Man*, which I thought was sad and boring, and during the day, and most evenings, I was taken care of by the Boltons. We would go to the same parties as Fonda, as if Fonda and I didn't really know each other, and he would watch me among his friends. He wanted to see how I behaved, or misbehaved. It was as if I was one of Pavlov's dogs, a guinea pig. He was forever finding out new things about me, but it was virtually impossible to find out much about him. *His* friends were usually in on the secret and all anyone said was: 'What a wonderful guy – he's great – I've never met a nicer man.' At the very worst someone might say he was a bore or a 'bit' wicked, when, really, he was something in between.

At the parties in those days literally everyone was there. The women wore elegant gowns and were sprayed in diamonds and suntans. The men were in dinner jackets. There was live music and everyone was polite and smiling. The whole season blended into a single memory – though one particular night stood out from all the rest.

It was a dinner party with everyone placed along a table that vanished into the distance. Our names were printed on white cards to mark our position. I was the 'Countess' Franchetti – inaccurate and unimportant to me, but dazzling to some of the nouveau riche people of Hollywood. I would only have been a countess had I married a count – like Lorian. My mother's title came from her parents, Count Rocca and the formidable Countess Moceniga Mocenigo. As Mama had married a mere baron, I inherited the title 'baronessa', which came in handy when I wanted to make an appointment with a new hairdresser, though little more. When I moved to America, Nanuck wrote me several letters addressed 'Baronessa Afdera Franchetti, New York', which never arrived. Had he written 'Mrs Henry Fonda, New York', I'm sure they would have.

So, there I was at dinner. Gary Cooper was opposite me with Mrs Cooper, somebody or other on my left and Hank Hathaway on my right – he was an old-time director, a rough, gruff, no-nonsense man and the least sociable person you could meet. He didn't know who the countess was and he couldn't have cared less.

I read his white place card and gave him the most innocent look.

'Ah, Hank?' I said. 'What a funny name. I think I met somebody else called Hank yesterday.'

'There's only one other Hank in the world and that's Hank Fonda,' he replied.

'Yes, yes – you mean Henry Fonda. Ooh, do tell me about him. I've just seen *War and Peace* in Italy, he's wonderful – you must tell me what he's like.'

'A pain in the arse,' Hank Hathaway said. 'A good man – but difficult.'

'Really, but why?' I was so pleased to hear something negative – there had to be a reason why all his wives left or committed suicide!

'He's hard to work with, that's the problem,' Hathaway replied.

The Coopers had followed every word. Gary Cooper was grinning and I thought he was marvellous. I adored his looks. He was a gentleman, not the best actor there ever was, but he had a certain magic. He said something, I smiled across the table, and his wife stared at me in the most awful way. Mrs Cooper was a socialite from one of those good American families, and I suppose at first, since my place card said I was a countess, she must have thought we had something in common – though she impressed me as a rather tough lady then and I liked her husband more, but eventually I came to realize that she was quite a woman.

The dinner passed, the floor was cleared and Gary Cooper asked me to dance. I was thrilled. I only came up to his navel, but we glided away with Mr Cooper still grinning. Hank Hathaway apparently took advantage of my absence to ask Mrs Cooper who I was.

When I got back to the table, Hank Hathaway was scarlet. He glared at me unpleasantly and said I was a dirty double-crosser.

'Who would think of playing a low-down trick like that?' he snarled. 'I hope Fonda's not going to marry a bitch like you, for his sake.'

I was caught out, but it was worth it. At least I knew I wasn't going to be partnered with someone the whole world thought of as St Francis of Assisi. Mr Hathaway lumbered away, and, when I did marry Fonda, it took me a whole year to win him over. Even so, he never really understood me and seemed to regard me as a creature from another planet, an Italian E.T.

Fonda was constantly offered roles and, because he was conscious of money, he hated to turn anything down. 'I'm just a humble country boy from Omaha, Nebraska,' he would say, though he became a legend, travelled everywhere and was married five times to beautiful, naughty or amusing women.

In the summer of 1956, he made an exception. He shut up shop, migrated to Hyannis Port, on Cape Cod, and moved Harriet Peacock and the three children into one of the lovely old wooden houses that sat perched above the water. It was surrounded by trees, smoke curled from a brick chimney, and there was a boat docked at the end of a small jetty. It was all very charming, like in the film, *On Golden Pond*, where Katharine Hepburn played mama to Hank's papa and Jane played the daughter. It was one of the rare occasions when Hank and Jane did appear on the same billing and, as coincidence would have it, the very first time was that summer, when the 'resting' Henry Fonda agreed to take a part in *The Male Animal*, with Jane and her apprentice group at the Dennis Playhouse.

That was before I arrived. When I did arrive, everyone was wearing tennis shoes and smiles and I felt like the alien Hank Hathaway thought I was. Father and daughter were openly displaying their affection, something I was never to see again, Harriet was mother hen, Amy was sparkling and Peter Fonda was all grins, pimples and superlatives. Everything was 'gre-at' and 'far out' and 'fan-tastic', including me, until we got to know each other better and then he decided that I was the worst thing to drop in on America since the bombs that fell on Pearl Harbor.

Harriet kept asking me what was wrong and I said nothing. I was just tired from all the flying and from Fonda's long series of little tests. This was the big one: I was there to meet the *bambini*. Jane and Peter were both very fond of Susan, which didn't help, and I had no intention of being the all-American stepmother. Jane was eighteen – and I had just had my twenty-third birthday. I was a woman of the world, like the adorable wicked queen to her naive and hapless Snow White. Jane was almost a child, but she was touched by a magic star – and she was learning, very, very fast.

Jane watched me, as did the rest of the family, but for different reasons. She was a nice, wholesome, puppy-fat teenager, ripening quickly, although even she didn't know what she was ripening into. A career in show business was still only vague in her mind and, at that time, her consuming interest was boys.

It must have been within the next six months that she discovered sex and then everything about her changed: her hormones, the look in her eyes. She slimmed down and became stunning. A real Narcissus; she would eat and then put her fingers down her throat and throw up so that she stayed thin. The final extra ounces of plumpness hung on around her ankles, which we managed to get rid of with the aid of a masseur.

We were then staying in a villa in Villefranche, in the South of France, where European heads were turning and Jane was now ready to take on the world. I knew then that whatever she decided to do, she would be successful. Apart from asking my advice about fat ankles, Jane asked me about contraception, though I'm sure she, being American, knew far more about those things than I did. I wasn't interested in where babies came from and my only firm belief was that the Pill caused cancer, which information I confidently passed on to her.

Peter in Cape Cod was watching me to see how I was with his dad (as Dad was watching to see how I was with his children) and for a while we struck up a lukewarm relationship. It quickly cooled. Peter and I were like a cat and a dog sharing the same sofa. We treated each other with a wary and feigned tolerance. At the beginning he told Fonda I was 'gre-at' and I tried to be nice because I had taken an instant dislike to him, for the pimples and the beers he drank from the can and the way he copied his father's habit of tilting back his chair and putting his feet up when he sat. I thought he was rather a bore.

Harriet was amiable, Amy bubbled like champagne and, though the famous Fonda eyes twinkled, it was still an ordeal facing the family *en masse*. I was sulky and tired from jet lag and blamed my sulks on the tennis shoes and the dark, choppy sea. Everything was grey, beige and dull and, as the appeal of each place seemed to grow the moment we left, I wanted to be back on Annibale's yacht in the warm, translucent Mediterranean. It was the end of the season. The sun had stopped being so unkindly hot and it was the best time to be in Italy. I looked up at the overcast New England sky and I withdrew silently into the clouds.

Fonda thought I was pining for lack of love and decided to cheer me up by making a formal proposal of marriage. It was sweet and completely mystifying, as if I was a seventeen-year-old virgin and he was the twenty-one-year-old boy next door. It was my third night at the house and, as on the other nights, we had sat together around the round table: the patriarch and the children. When Harriet and Jane cleared the dishes, we walked out on the jetty and one of my high heels got stuck between the planks. I screamed; it was the last straw. A sliver of moon was flitting through the mist. There were stars high above. It was a scene from a B movie. Hank swept me into his arms.

'Let's get married,' he said.

'No, I don't want to,' I gasped.

'All right,' he replied.

'Well, let's think it over ...'

'All right,' he said again.

Thus it continued. I said no when I meant to say yes, and Fonda was clever enough to know what I meant. We kissed. It was funny and romantic and no more was said. That was typical of us, nothing was ever said.

Another day passed. It was time for me to return to Rome and only one more thing happened that I can remember – something I'm sure Jane Fonda has forgotten. She had become intrigued by my perfume.

'It really is extraordinary,' she said. 'I've never known anything so beautiful.'

Fonda glanced over and smiled.

'What's the brand?' he asked.

'It's Arpège,' I replied.

Fonda then went off quietly and bought two tiny bottles, one for each of us. Jane put it on her wrists and dabbed it behind her ears and stood there aghast: on her it had a completely different odour – not disagreeable, but entirely different.

There was one other time that my perfume pleased another woman's nose – but then, I forgot the make, as well as my English. It was at the opening of an art exhibition featuring a new portrait of Mrs Thatcher – and I was suddenly face to face with the lady herself.

'What nice perfume you're wearing,' she said. 'What is it?'

'I don't know, I can't hear it.'

'The word is *smell*,' she said sternly.

'I can't smell it, either,' I said, and shrugged.

From Cape Cod I returned to Rome to find everybody, even that outrageous playboy the King of the Bidets, suddenly feeling sorry for Augusto. The social air was icy and, for the first time in my life, I felt alone.

To make matters worse, I began receiving a stream of letters and cables not only from Fonda but also from Peter, who was still in the 'gre-at' phase, and kept finding awful cards: Dear Stepmother, Future

Mother's Day, all sorts. It upset me terribly. Jane Fonda didn't write, of course, although her father said she missed me. 'Your perfume is everywhere and your presence is haunting us all,' he reported. Jane was at a vulnerable age and, for a while, I was the one she decided to model herself on. That would change, endlessly change. Jane was a most accomplished chameleon, as I was soon to discover.

I was soon discontented with life in Rome and just over a month later I was buckled once more into an aeroplane seat and on my way to spend Thanksgiving in America with Fonda, Jimmy Stewart and Jimmy's wife, Gloria, who was divine.

It was my first Thanksgiving and I had to learn all about that dreadful thing called turkey. It was so enormous, you have to cook it for hours and then you have to eat it for hours, and you can't say no because the ceremony is as sacred a ritual in America as taking holy mass at Christmas. The whole awesome experience made my heart pound: everyone patting this white, naked monster – and then putting things in its behind – breadcrumbs and nuts, mysterious herbs, bits of old sausage. Even worse, you have to say how marvellous it is or everyone will be insulted.

Eating the turkey was unpleasant enough, but what to me seemed the very pinnacle of vulgarity was that we had to eat it again the next day, and the day after, and the day after – cold with a salad, in sandwiches, boiled in a hot pot, in soups, pâtés, preserves, curried. It's obvious why they only have it once a year. They eat it until they're sick of it. Everyone indulges, but there is a limit, even to one's own pleasures.

On the positive side, Jimmy Stewart and Gloria were simply marvellous. He was like Fonda; established, old school. I considered Fonda the better actor, but Jimmy had that special something that made him good to look at on the screen.

Gloria Stewart had a great sense of humour and I adored her. She taught me how to do *petit point* when I was trying to be the good wife. We went to the Farmer's Market and bought cottons and things, the outing always more important than the embroidered doilies I never made. Thank God. If I had, what would Fonda have done with them? The little excursions were just an excuse for me to listen to Gloria's amazing stories, usually about children, which made them vaguely esoteric. Gloria was funny, but she was also sensible and a good friend. She said I should think carefully before I married Fonda – for the sake of us both. She had already been through a bad marriage and realized how lucky she was to be with James Stewart.

'You have to suffer a bit before you can appreciate a man like Fonda,' she added.

She was right, but by the time I knew she was right, it was too late. I was hungry and undisciplined. Each experience was just a stepping-stone that I touched on before racing to the next. When there was snow on the trees in Manhattan, I wanted to be on a beach somewhere; on the most perfect sunny day I dreamed of clouds and thunderstorms; when I was reading a book I wanted to be out dancing and when I was dancing I wanted to be on my own with a book. I suppose I had always had so much that I didn't know what I really wanted.

Thanksgiving passed. The turkey wishbones were thrown away and I doped myself up for the flight back to Rome. It was almost Christmas, the season of goodwill to all mankind and womankind, except me. Most of my acquaintances had now decided that I was far too capricious, a view I endorsed by appearing more careless and carefree than usual. It was a ploy, but it didn't work. I dined with different beaux, but by the time the candles had burned down in their holders and the waiters were about to serve the cheese, I was ready to run home for my nightly call from East 74th.

The same good friends who thought I had handled the break with Augusto badly now thought I was being unfair to Henry Fonda. I was, but I wasn't. I was unsure and I had to meet as many people as possible to make up my mind. Who would buy a bottle of perfume without first opening the bottle? I was testing myself, as well as the people around me. Augusto, even at that late stage, would have taken me back; he still believed my feelings for Fonda were mere infatuation. There were others, boys and men I had known all my life and whom I or my sister had considered for husbands. But it was marriage itself I feared.

Annibale Scotti, dear man that he is, could see I was miserable, although I continued to play the games we had always played.

'Now, what are you going to do about Henry Fonda?' he would ask.

'Henry Fonda? I don't even know him.'

'But I saw him in New York!'

'Did you?'

'You know I did.'

'On Broadway?'

'No, at the bar in the Hotel Warwick.'

'Really?'

His bottom lip dropped and I pretended to be happy. Annibale was enchanting. All my life I had only told him lies.

It was a relief from the confusion, augmented now by the little whispers being breathed in my ear. As Augusto had once been told that I was seeing Fonda, people delighted in telling me that Fonda was seeing someone else. I didn't say anything to him directly, but the next time I said how uncertain I was about our getting married, he responded by saying: 'Okay, that's fine, that's life ...'

I was free – and I went for days wondering what I was going to do with my freedom. I knew I was making a mess of everything. I felt like a kite without a string, drifting on the breeze. I didn't want to be tied down, but I needed something. I was afraid of becoming more of a kite and I was terrified of having the string attached. There was always the yin and the yang, a paradox, and I was always trapped somewhere in between.

Mama was by now more eccentric than ever; Lorian played the role of observer; what I needed and never had was a father. I felt like a pariah in Italy, but that would pass and wasn't so important. My dilemma was deeper than that, something intangible; my doubts were purely instinctive. America was a fresh fall of snow and I simply couldn't see my footsteps printing a path over its surface. The Fondas seemed so pure and perfect, new-born souls, unlike me, with roots that were hidden in the dark earth of my Gothic past. I liked Fonda, I loved him in my way, but I was like a bird that needed freedom and self-will unlike a kite that moves with the will of the wind.

Fonda, youthful and boyish though he was, was a part of something that was already established – and I belonged to all that was coming. It was the genesis of a new era. The 1960s were barely on the horizon, but I could taste the first breath of the hurricane. I could see it on canvases, I could hear it in the music. There was something exciting in the eyes of young people – Jane Fonda had it, for sure. The old restraints were vanishing, but it took me all those months back in Italy to see that Fonda, as well as being a harbour, would also be a gateway to the new world that was coming. I was afraid of marriage, that little golden ring like the first bar of a cage. But, while marriage can be a prison, it can also be an escape, for me an escape from my crazy family.

Life as I had known it was dying. I was suffering the pains of rebirth. I was a statue being released from its mould and I entered life knowing nothing except one thing: Henry Fonda did love me – and from that cornerstone we would build something.

All these thoughts washed through me like a changing tide and, while my mind was still unsettled, a cable arrived from Fonda one morning which finally put an end to my hesitation. On it were the words: LET'S NOT LOSE TIME STOP DO IT STOP HANK.

I packed my bags, I booked a flight and was almost on the point of leaving when Nanuck appeared from Venice to play out his role as the head of the family. He had been incited by Mama, who had peered through the mists of her madness to announce that she didn't want her youngest daughter to marry a man who had been married so many times before, who had grown-up children and who wasn't a Catholic. It was a sudden decision and a complete turn-around from the view she had after Fonda had written her a long, beautiful letter asking for my hand. She had said yes then and regretted it later; now, as Nanuck saw everything as either black or white, he decided that he had a duty to perform and duly arrived to perform it.

He slammed the door.

'I hear you're going to America,' he said. 'Is it true?'

'Yes, it is.'

'And you're going to marry this actor?'

'Yes, I am.'

'Mama doesn't want you to marry him.'

'Well, I'm going to.'

'Oh no you're not,' he said, in the same flat, loud voice.

'Oh yes I am,' I replied. I knew Nanuck and I knew what was coming. Bang. Bang. He slapped me on both cheeks.

'Now, for the last time,' he said. 'Are you going to marry this actor?'

'Yes, I am ... whatever happens.'

Bang. Bang. He hit me once again. I cried. And that was that. Nanuck was always a bit eccentric and, where others may have found him hard to understand, I shared the same confused, tangled roots, as well as an affinity for outbursts of irrational behaviour. We loved each other dearly, even though the expression of that love was apt to be peculiar. I wasn't upset. Nanuck had done what he considered was the right thing to do, and went back to Venice without thinking any more about it. He had other things on his mind.

While I had been falling in love with Henry Fonda – whatever games I played, I was too much of a romantic not to be in love with the man I married – my brother was falling for a Cuban débutante by the name of Kristina, spelt with an ominous K. She was a member of one of the most celebrated families in the dying days before Castro and moved with the crowd that gathered at Hemingway's home, the Finca Vigia, though Papa himself couldn't bear her. He thought she was spoilt and selfish, yet very beautiful – the only reason he admitted her. Unlike Papa, a man of vast experience, Nanuck and his best friend, Gianfranco Ivancich, who owned a large estate next to the Franchetti land, saw only Kristina's dark eyes and sensual charms. Both were greatly enamoured, but Nanuck was already married and had no option but to stand aside. Gianfranco led her up the aisle and back to Venice. Thus began the saga that was to continue over the years and goes on to this very day.

In many ways, the story all began in Nanuck's childhood. He was surrounded by women – servants and sisters – but for all the love directed at him, his one great love was for Mama: she was older, as indeed was Laura, who became his wife when my brother was just nineteen.

Laura was very different from us, in spite of coming from a very ancient and well-established family. She was born a Dona delle Rose, a family which had produced three doges; she was well bred and well schooled, but was not very sophisticated. She saw everything in terms of money, which is strange, because people with money don't usually think about it.

Laura had had three children and was a very good mother. They came in quick succession before Nanuck met Kristina and decided that she was the right woman for him. Gianfranco had married her – Kristina had three children by him – but Nanuck was always close by. The two couples were together constantly. The six children grew up virtually as one family, but when Kristina became pregnant with her fourth, she announced that her love-child belonged to Nanuck.

The two women drew swords and their duel scandalized Venice. They were like two fishwives, yelling the most obscene abuse and even throwing things whenever they met in the narrow streets of the city. Laura told her children that if they should see Kristina they were to spit at her. She really was common – and as for the beautiful débutante, she could give as good as she got.

Nanuck and Gianfranco didn't take too much notice of it all. They were a pair of hard-drinking hunting men and, when the two women fought, they disappeared – together. They remained the best of friends and I'm sure that even now not a day goes by without Gianfranco lighting a candle to Nanuck. Gianfranco divorced Kristina, Nanuck divorced Laura, and then Nanuck and Kristina were married. She finally had what she wanted: she was now Baronessa Kristina Franchetti.

The marriage was full of passion, violence and, of course, children. After having a boy, Kristina gave birth to a girl and, with the other six, that made eight children that Nanuck had to support.

They set up home in Treviso and the new Baronessa took command of the wheel, guiding the household like the *Titanic* to its doom. All the flowers in the garden died. The trees fell down. The servants packed their belongings and left. Kristina – I'm sure it had something to do with that K – was like a steamroller, crushing everything, even our fond memories.

The house was a part of us, as important as one's heart. It had come to be known as the Villa Franchetti. It was really three houses in one, like a Roman temple, and certainly it was the temple of our souls and our past. It was bought originally for my father's grandmother as part of her dowry. She was a Rothschild, from the famous line of German financiers, and Jewish, as indeed was my own family until comparatively recent times. They were originally Franks, from which the name Franchetti derives, a tribe of merchants who followed the crusades and eventually settled in North Africa. There, as was the custom of the time, they traded in everything from gold and gemstones to spices and slaves. They moved their business to Venice during the Renaissance and during the next two centuries the Jewish sons married Catholic girls and their children became good Italians. They acquired a title and a family crest and, slowly, frittered away a fortune.

The house was the last symbol of the wealth that once was and, when the servants left, even that began to fall down. It was then that the new Baronessa decided that she wanted to move the twenty-five miles from the country to Venice, and Nanuck agreed – as Nanuck always agreed to everything. The house that had sheltered us for four generations was sold and has since become an architectural college. The museum that

Papa had stocked after his many expeditions was given away as a gift. Generosity runs through Nanuck like the blood in his veins: he made various other donations and then purchased the main floor in the Barbaro, an ancient palace that has been converted into a few opulent apartments. It is an elegant, imposing building with a façade that makes sculptured shadows on the Grand Canal and stands – by accident or design – immediately next to the Palazzo Franchetti. The view across the water to these two fine palaces is the most painted and photographed scene in Venice, the ideal spot for Kristina – although, like everything else, the palazzo no longer has any connection with my family. My father sold it to fund one of his expeditions.

The family wealth was dwindling then and has dwindled ever since, so that now, though the various branches of the family are by no means poor, the money they have they work for, an activity that was once unknown to us.

Gloria Stewart's wise words on suffering were true, but only in a limited sense. I had never really wanted for anything, but I was born with a foot in two worlds. I had witnessed the old world of my fated family as it stumbled into the future. In our ranks we had explorers, composers and innovators, the pursuits of the privileged. Now there are lawyers, publishers and politicians, vocations just as valid, but not so exotic.

Nanuck is from the old world and, like our Papa, has no aptitude with money. After buying the apartment for his wife, he used the rest of his capital to begin a fish farm on a part of his lands at San Gaetano. It was an enormous and immensely complex scheme: vast pools of little fishes, a labyrinth of snaking tubes, long, low buildings for scores of foreign scientists, tall view towers. It was like being at Cape Kennedy. A lot of work went into it. We all should have become rich again and lived happily ever after. But Nanuck was touched by the Franchetti eccentricity (or the curse that had been put on Mama by an Abyssinian princess – another story) and somehow, something went wrong. All male fish were born one year, all females the next. The scientists fled, the fish farm became a ghost town and the banks, of course, were insufferable. Nanuck carried on by borrowing more money – he is the sort of man who only has to ask and his friends pull out their cheque books. But that, his joy, was also his undoing. In the end, he lost it all – but I still love him.

Kristina was so bitter, she locked her husband out and locked herself in. She lived in an apartment as big as a palace, that once was a palace. The servants left and, while one daughter remained to cook her meals, Nanuck commenced his new life, moving around the homes of his other children. It was fortunate that he had so many.

Nanuck is a man who never worried about his appearance. He wore battered shoes and crumpled jackets, yet still managed to look noble. Once his nonchalance was a source of amusement; now, there is nothing amusing about it at all. It makes me sad and it makes me wonder. I'm not religious, but if there is a God, I'm sure there is a fault on the line that links Him with us. Simba died so young; Papa was killed; Mama was widowed in her thirties and had a thoroughly complicated life; Nanuck married two women with terrible tongues and went deaf so that he didn't have to listen to them; Lorian has lost a son and one of her daughters lost a husband. That leaves me, with my laughter and a face that shows no suffering. Fortunate me, who always gave the impression of having everything, the frivolous free spirit who was always quietly watching – usually through dark glasses, like the Arabs, so that people could see my expression, but not my eyes.

I was far too self-critical and analytical not to be aware of what was going on around me and around the world, but rarely did I allow my deepest thoughts to rise to my lips. Instead, I kept my thoughts hidden and I hid myself behind a smile. I was gay and witty, perhaps naughty and outrageous, and always, always I was me. I was constantly looking for something, constantly running away from something, and, if you were running in 1957, there was only one place to run to: New York.

4 . Venice in Manhattan

As the car made its way through the glossy wet streets of Rome, I peered from the window and wondered when I would be back. I never seemed to stay anywhere for long. I had finally pushed all doubts from my mind and was sitting beside my sister as her car hurried to the airport.

The driver took care of the luggage. We were late and there was only a short while for Lorian and me to say our farewells. She planted herself before me, on her arm a bag that she had carried throughout the journey. Her eyes held an amused, faintly wicked smile and her lips were as straight and precisely drawn as a Modigliani. People flooded around us, as if we were rocks in the middle of a stream. Lorian didn't appear to notice them. She was too busy studying me.

'Well, Afdera, you've managed to make up your mind,' she said. It was a statement, not a question, and she spoke in English, as if in deference to the custom at table: it didn't so much matter what you did and said, as long as one was discreet in front of the servants – a discretion rarely for the sake of secrecy, but because the servants were always assumed to be easily upset.

I shrugged.

'Did you manage to tell Augusto that you were going to marry Henry Fonda?'

'Not exactly, it's not easy,' I answered.

The thin line of her lips changed shape. 'I'll tell him when I get back to Rome.'

'Thank you, Lorian, you can be so helpful,' I said; especially if there's some little intrigue, I thought, although I kept that bit quiet.

She raised her eyebrows. The suitcases had trundled away on the conveyor belt.

'You can still change your mind and come back tomorrow if you want to,' Lorian declared evenly.

Once more, I didn't reply. I was just pleased that my sister was being so supportive. She was always for me and equally against me, as if, like our whole family, she was afraid of showing too much affection.

I remember once when I was a little girl of eight or nine, it was time for me to go to bed and I suddenly had this strange urge. I just put my arms around my mother and kissed her on the lips. She pushed me away. 'Don't you ever, ever do that again,' she said angrily. 'Not to anyone.'

It came back to mind that moment at the airport. We concealed what love we had. We buried it deeper and deeper until we forgot where it was. It was true of both of us. We understood each other far better than we wanted to, or cared to admit.

I glanced up at the large clock on the wall. It was time for me to go through passport control. I went to kiss Lorian's cheeks, but she pulled away and told me to wait. On her lips now was the tiniest of smiles. She opened the bag she had been holding so tightly and then produced her wedding gifts: surprises, extraordinary things – a miniature pair of opera glasses in ivory – 'for seeing near and far,' she said; there was a watch with an extra dial that gave the times all over the world, so I would always know what time it was in Italy; and a photograph in a silver frame that had been taken at Lorian's wedding and showed the two of us with Nanuck and Simba, our beloved Simba, the one Franchetti who wasn't afraid of her feelings.

Tears began to mist my eyes and, as if she had been prepared for it, Lorian pulled out her handkerchief.

'Something borrowed,' she said and gave it to me. 'It's the tradition.'

I stared back at my sister. I was speechless. I felt happy, but peculiar. Lorian was always so tricky. I had the feeling that the act had yet to reach its finale – and I was right. Lorian's little smile grew bigger and then, finally, she opened her purse and gave me a cheque, the sum being the exact cost of a one-way air ticket from New York to Rome – 'just in case'.

We embraced and Lorian turned away. Her driver was waiting patiently at the exit door and she glided towards him like a great liner on the ocean.

I don't know what it was I drank, but whatever it was, I gulped it down and by the time I arrived in New York I felt as if I was looking through the wrong end of my ivory opera glasses. I was completely sloshed. Fonda took me home. He had booked himself into an hotel for good luck, but ended up sitting there all night, holding my hand and saying comforting words. I just cried ... cried and cried and cried. I was gaining the world, but I was losing just a little bit of me.

The Peacocks flew in from Nebraska with Peter the following morning – Friday, 10 March 1957. I was puffy and red-eyed, Peter Fonda had a face like a winter's night, Jane arrived from Vassar, blooming – it was six months after Cape Cod and she was another person – Jack was jolly, Harriet was Harriet; and then the judge turned up with his good humour and good advice. He was an elderly, white-haired Jewish man from New Jersey who told us that none of the couples he had married had ever been divorced.

It was a funny word to hear at a marriage ceremony – especially as the judge didn't know how touch and go it had been. Even at that moment I felt just a little guilty: my bouquet was made up from flowers that had been sent by Renaldito Herrera.

We stood there in the library at East 74th, kicking our heels and looking at each other. The judge was fiddling about and getting ready, when Jane broke the tension and told us what had happened on her way from the station.

'I climbed into a taxi and you'll never guess what the driver said.' She paused – New York taxi drivers are divinely chatty. Jane grinned and then added: 'He said: "I see that Henry Fonda's getting married again ... for the fourth time." "Really?" "Yea, it's in all the papers – he's marrying some Italian broad."'

Everyone laughed. I don't know if it was true or not – Jane loved to exaggerate – but it broke the ice and it was the perfect thing to say. She was looking at me – but she was worried about her Papa. It was some time later that Peter told us that when he had asked for a few days' leave from school to attend his father's wedding, the headmaster responded by saying how disgusting and un-Christian it was for a man to marry so many times. At that, Peter claimed, he punched him on the nose.

So, the tension had been broken. Fonda gripped my hand, Peter moved forward to act as his father's best man, and the performance began. I had steeled myself for it, though at the words 'Till death do you part' my flesh crawled with goose pimples and I almost burst into tears. I always cry at weddings and never at funerals. The final words of the ceremony were said. There was a pause.

It was done.

The corks popped and we clinked glasses. It was nice when everyone disappeared and we were left on our own. Fonda and I always had our best times when no one else was around.

The day went, the night went, Fonda was up with the larks and when I got up and wandered across the room to look out on the world as a Fonda instead of a Franchetti, I was just in time to see a corpse being shuttled into the funeral parlour right opposite the house. I screamed. I don't think I ever quite recovered from it.

'Hank ...' – I called him Hank in the early days – 'It's horrible ... I want to move.'

He laughed. We didn't move, but the following week we had an air-conditioning unit installed and the window that looked out on the funeral parlour was blocked up.

It was a new life and it began with a fleeting glimpse of death. It could have been something out of Nietzsche, and it seemed as if it had been arranged for my eyes alone, as Fonda seemed subtly linked to the flute players in Pamplona. There were always lessons for the learning and, with Henry Fonda, you just never knew. He was many men and was interested in many things. He would stand on his head every morning for five minutes and then go through a whole series of yoga postures, something that everyone does now and that the Chinese and Japanese have been doing since the world began, but not many middle-aged Americans were doing in 1957.

Fonda had close friends in the highest of high places, but he could drift like an air bubble from their world and be just as comfortable with Ginsberg, Kerouac and the beat art generation that was suddenly gathering around 47th Street, where Andy Warhol had his studio. '*You have to suffer to appreciate a man like Fonda*'... I had suffered, but not in love. That was to come.

The cadaver, dressed better than anyone I see in London these days – except some of the chauffeurs – was quickly out of sight and out of mind. If the experience was a little upsetting, it was nothing compared with what happened two hours later when we arrived at the airport and I stared up at our mode of transport. It was a Walt Disney invention or worse. I was stupefied with disbelief. It wasn't a normal aircraft, but some terrible hybrid, a pterodactyl with a box slung below its belly –

and it was there, in that box, that we were supposed to sit.

'I'm not getting in that,' I gasped.

'But it's only for half an hour,' Fonda replied.

'I don't care if it's for half a second, I'm not going.'

'Afdera?'

'Why don't we go to the Ritz?' I suggested. 'Or the Waldorf?'

'Afdera?'

'Hank?'

We both stood our ground. The sky darkened, the row of propellers groaned into life and the faint fall of snow that was in the air started to whip itself into a wild, frenzied blizzard. Someone started to shout from the oval doorway above us, although we could not hear a word. However, I did hear Fonda's cough, and it was then that I saw my choices trickling away. He had been up all night, poor thing, and now he had a fever. It was the only time he was ever ill in the whole of his life. I either had to climb on board that death trap of a flying-machine or stand there and watch my new husband get a dose of pneumonia.

'Afdera?'

I shook my head and shouted into the wind: 'Come on then,' I said. 'Let's get it over with.'

We climbed the stairs, the door shut out the raging blizzard, and as the weird winged monster lifted into the sky I said my prayers. Like Dali, I practise without being a believer.

That thirty-minute journey took us from New York over the mountains to Mont Tremblant, in Quebec, where we were to have a two-day honeymoon in a mountain chalet that turned out to be cold and draughty, before Fonda rushed back to begin work on a new film, *Stage Struck*, with Susan Strasberg, directed by his old friend Sidney Lumet. It was nice to be on our own, but it would have been just as nice at the Ritz.

We sat there, huddled round a fire with warm fronts and icy backs. Fonda nursed a head cold, while, halfway across the world, Lorian was nursing Augusto Torlonia. He had finally learnt that I had married Fonda from a newspaper, not from my sister – though even then he still refused to believe it. He went straight to Piazza Lovatelli and, when Lorian confirmed it was true, in a moment of high drama he took four Mogadons plus two aspirins and slept around the clock on Lorian's sofa.

Now, I can shed a tear for Augusto, although on my honeymoon all

Mama on her travels through Africa after Papa's death
ABOVE RIGHT Papa in Ethiopia
RIGHT Me aged about fifteen months
BELOW (*Back row, left to right*) Uncle Nico Mocenigo, Mama,
Countess Soranzo, my godmother Constanza Mocenigo,
Duke Amedeo D'Aosta with my brother Nanuck; (*front row*)
my sister Lorian, Countess Marcello, me, Grandmama
Mocenigo and my sister Simba

Me, Mama holding Nanuck's first son Alberto and Lorian with a portrait of Papa in front of the Afdera volcano and a sculpture of Grandmama Mocenigo in the background

LEFT Holding my dog Towser
BELOW LEFT Simba during the war
BELOW With Annibale Scotti

Palazzo Franchetti (*left*), where Papa was brought up, and Palazzo Barbero , next to it, where Nanuck now lives, Grand Canal, Venice

With Nanuck after a duck shoot at San Gaetano

OPPOSITE ABOVE Lunching with Mary and Ernest Hemingway in Spain, photographed by Fonda
OPPOSITE BELOW Fonda and I on the set of *The Tin Star*

TOP Fonda with Audrey Hepburn, Mel Ferrer and Gary Cooper in Paris, photographed by me

ABOVE LEFT On holiday in Toledo, Spain
ABOVE RIGHT On honeymoon with Fonda in Canada

Collecting the Golden Bear Award in Berlin for 'Twelve Angry Men'

Amy

Amy

Amy

Jane and I discussing the facts of life

Peter and Jane

OPPOSITE At a party with Mrs Jack Heinz, Salvador Dali, a friend and Gala Dali
The Fondas entertaining: Gary Cooper; Gregory Peck with Christopher Isherwood and Ivan
Moffat in the background at a Kennedy campaign party at our home; Merle Oberon; Frank
Sinatra

In our house in New York

my tears had dried up and, when I wasn't sitting in front of the fire, I
was staring at my puffy eyes and swollen face in the mirror. I looked so
bad that when the wedding photographs appeared, on an impulse, I
took a pair of nail scissors and cut my eyes out of every one. It was an
odd thing to do, on reflection, though at the time it made perfect sense!

Three days later, we were back home at East 74th, where I wandered
through the house thinking about *mobilia* – furniture. The beloved Jack
Peacock had done the house in such an ugly way that describing now
how I felt then is almost impossible. It wasn't a case of good taste or
bad taste; there was no taste at all. Imagine a dentist's waiting-room,
or the Hilton, Nebraska, circa 1950. The things that Jack had acquired
to make me feel comfortable were by no means cheap, they were
the modern things one might buy at Macy's, the dream of successful
plumbers, perhaps, or bus drivers newly arrived from the Urals. But Mr
Fonda? And the new Mrs Fonda? Certainly not.

Thank goodness Fonda had taken up painting as a hobby and so
there were some of his charming still lifes around the flat – a few of
which I still treasure; I grouped them together so that they provided at
least one nice feature in our home.

The spacious rooms were filled with peculiar objects that I quickly
moved out, though when it came to the dining-room, it was so divinely
bizarre I just didn't have the heart to touch it. It was Jack Peacock's
magnum opus, his vision of Venetian splendour – and something Fellini
might have used for one of his orgy scenes: giant mirrors, chandeliers,
copies of Italian bureaux. It was unbelievable. All around the room
were curling things, hanging things and everything in fake gold. It was
hideous, yet so quaintly diverting that I allowed it to remain unchanged
for a whole year.

While I moved the other bits and pieces out, I drew mental pictures
of where the replacements were going to go. Luckily, in the months
before I left Rome I had accumulated a mass of goods mainly from a
new and exciting gallery run by Ruggero Nuvolari, one of the friends
who stuck by me when the rest of Rome was turning a cold shoulder.
I had purchased chairs, tables, cabinets, and a beautiful wooden figure
that came originally from Naples. Curtains were being made by Mama's
curtain maker in Treviso. I had virtually everything I required except a
bed and that, for purely aesthetic reasons, had to be special. In Venice
hundreds of years ago, the daughters of poor people made their bridal

bed in *papier mâché*, a style called *arte povera* and now, of course, collectors' pieces that cost a small fortune. That was what I wanted and Ruggero Nuvolari scoured the whole of Italy until he found one.

Everything was packed into crates and shipped to New York with my precious Fidalma and her new husband, Giuseppe, a short, stocky man with a lot of hair and all the cunning and good sense of a peasant.

I waited impatiently for weeks and finally, before I went mad, the delivery note appeared in the afternoon mail, which fitted into my plan of action like a key in the appropriate lock. I didn't breathe a word to Fonda until the following morning, although then my little request threw him completely off balance.

'Why don't you come home a bit later this evening, Hank?' I suggested.

'Later? But why? Whatever for?'

'Well, I don't know. It doesn't matter why!'

We stood there in the empty hallway, me with a straight face and Fonda suddenly wearing the puzzled look that came over him the very first time we met ... *can you pass the salt, please ... can you pass the pepper, please ...*

Fonda took a step forward. 'Is there anything wrong, Afdera? Can I do anything?' he said.

'No, nothing's wrong. Just come home late tonight,' I replied.

I looked angry and didn't explain. It was the only thing I could do. Fonda had rehearsals all day, but would always rush home at six o'clock for supper.

'You're sure?' he pressed.

'Yes,' I said in an exasperated voice. 'Go to work and don't come home until nine o'clock.'

'Nine?'

'Please.'

He turned his head on to one side, shrugged his shoulders and finally agreed.

I ushered him out of the house and rushed straight for the telephone. I called the customs agent and the transport company and arranged to have everything delivered – the bills, naturally, at a later date.

'Oh, and one more thing,' I told the transport manager. 'I want twenty-five men to help.'

'Twenty-five men? You putting me on, lady?' he said, or words to that effect.

'Indeed I'm not,' I answered in my best English. 'I've got a lot of work to do.'

'It's going to cost.'

'It doesn't matter what it costs. It's very urgent.'

'Okay, ma'am,' he paused. 'This is Mrs *Henry* Fonda I'm talking to, is it?'

'The fourth,' I said. 'And make sure you send careful men, I don't want anything broken.'

'Don't worry, I'll send the best.'

He hung up. An hour later, the trucks were parked outside. The helpers materialized, all broad-shouldered and grinning, and, with me like a general at the dawn of an important battle, we went to work. It was a production line. The crates were opened with great care and the contents were carried into the house, upstairs, through corridors, into one room and then out again. Everything was teased and tested into place. My skills are rather few but, even if I say so myself, my interiors are quite passable. Fidalma polished and fussed and adored everything; Giuseppe lifted only the heaviest things. He was as tough as nails and I'm sure by now he's the head of the Mafia.

We drank coffee and ate sandwiches. Everything was in, everything was shuffled about, and by the time the sun was slipping below the tall Manhattan buildings, it was done – except for one last, tiny detail: Fidalma and Giuseppe changed into green uniforms that made them look like Austrian mountain climbers, as bizarre as the dining-room, the doors of which were tightly closed. My Italian servants were from the south and both were so short and funny, I couldn't resist making them even funnier. The lamps threw out a warm amber glow, every surface shone, every casually dropped magazine had been dropped in its place. Even the curtains fitted perfectly.

I let out an enormous sigh. The glass-domed clock chimed the hour of nine, and at two minutes past the master appeared.

Naturally, I didn't say a word. Fidalma was bursting to say something, but she didn't know a scrap of English, and Henry Fonda didn't speak Italian.

'I don't believe it,' he finally gasped. 'I really don't believe it.'

I took my glasses off and looked thoroughly surprised.

'How did you do it? It's sensational, it's a miracle, it's fantastic.' He wandered from room to room, waving his arms around as if he was searching for more adjectives. 'It's breathtaking, it's phenomenal, it's fabulous ...'

He was discovering a side of my character that he had never seen before and, once shown, he was never to see again. He loved the way it had all been arranged: it was so un-American, a mishmash, highly organized to appear cosy and disorganized – books piled on tables, single blooms in tall vases, paintings all randomly, carefully, positioned. In those days, I thought it was very important to have it all just right – and it was.

Jane, when she saw the changes, was pleasantly surprised and Peter made a noise like *gee wow*. I never listened to Peter and Fonda only pretended to. He so obviously adored his daughter that he was forever over-compensating and being over-protective towards his son. Jane, safe under her magic star, understood Papa's dilemma and loved him for it even more.

Jane didn't seem to resent me, although she knew that I wasn't going to be the nice cosy little wife who was always at home. Still, we got on rather well – and even better from the distance of the apartment she moved into with a new boyfriend within a few months of my arrival. Peter was shuffled away to Nebraska, where he could get all the attention he needed from his aunt and uncle.

I was horrible to Peter, truly horrible, and for that I think he was always grateful. He simply loved to feel sorry for himself and I gave him good reason. He was so in the shadow of his father and sister, he did everything he could to be in the centre and never was. All his friends seemed to commit suicide, and once he actually tried to shoot himself. Like everything else, that went wrong as well. Hank and Jane made a fuss over him but, like the Franchettis, the Fondas weren't very good at it.

When I had suggested that Peter be sent to the Peacocks, Fonda readily agreed. It was a great mistake, to my mind, because eventually I didn't respect him for it. Fonda was still in the besotted stage, as only an older man can be with a younger woman, and often it got on my nerves. Everything I had bought in Italy he loved, but a bit too much: at the time, if I had told him that *la merde* was caviar, he would have eaten it. This didn't last, of course, but the patterns we make have a habit of returning and, in some ways, it blighted our marriage right from the start. He was the legend, but also a man – and with all the normal weaknesses.

* * *

56

After our disastrous two-day honeymoon in Canada, Fonda promised to take the summer off – the second in a row – and have a proper honeymoon in Europe. He finished filming *Stage Struck*, was immediately offered and half agreed to do a play by Bill Gibson called *Two for the Seesaw* – it was one of the few we read together – and then off we set – not alone, like any other honeymoon, but with Jane and Peter and a gang of their friends, with Amy and her nurse and with Fidalma and Giuseppe. It was a bit like a travelling circus.

Fonda rented a villa in Cap Ferrat, near the port of Villefranche, and there we settled into a summer woven through with sunshine and society. The Riviera turned out to be full of people I knew – it would be easier to say who wasn't there rather than who was. The Fiat boss Gianni Agnelli and his wife Marella were our nearest neighbours, hovering on the clifftops above up in La Leopolda, a magnificent summer house set in a froth of greenery. Inside was a dreamy, Second Empire elegance where the ghosts of Zelda and F. Scott Fitzgerald would have felt most at home. We exchanged dinner invitations. Fonda was terribly popular and wherever Jane went, interested eyes were sure to follow. She was really awed by her sudden blossoming but, as the actress she would soon become, she took everything in her stride.

Further round the craggy coastline at Monte Carlo, the Onassis boat dominated the harbour. The parties on board were frequent, which made the search for new costumes consuming. I had become fond of the designs by Valentino, often high necked and low backed, quite beautiful with a suntan.

I was thus attired and as short-sighted as always when one evening, strolling alone on the deck, I turned a corner and bumped straight into the famous square bulk of Winston Churchill. He took his cigar from his mouth and was about to speak, but I backed quickly away. I didn't want to make the same *faux pas* as my sister Lorian, who was once photographed with Churchill in Venice. It was a festival and she was a young débutante, but neither her age nor the innocence of the occasion prevented one newspaper from asking the question: is Signorina Franchetti unaware of who killed her father?

I vanished into the shadows and the thought flickered only briefly in my mind. There were other things to think about: rumours that Aristotle Onassis was seeing Maria Callas were being whispered over champagne glasses. I was sure this was true because Tina Onassis was flirting with

Renaldito Herrera. They visited us secretly at Cap Ferrat and it was so romantic it made me wistful for the days before Fonda and I were married. I was still a new bride, but I had a sneaking feeling that, although good times were ahead, the very best times were already behind us. Tina, freed from the giant aura of Aristotle, was wonderful. She would say whatever came into her head in a most refreshing way. In the end, she was a tragic figure, but that summer she was a free spirit and someone I admired. Her daughter Christina was also around, a dark, peculiar little girl.

Another visitor to the house was Greta Garbo, who would telephone to make sure no one else was there and then turn up wearing her bath robe, the pockets stuffed with a rubber swimming hat and lots of packets of cigarettes. George Schlee, her companion, would be with her, his dark eyes roaming everywhere, like the hands of a magician. I kept thinking that he was sitting there imagining Garbo and me in bed together. She was interested in me and made that obvious, although not for the reasons her companion appeared to be conjuring up. Like a lot of people in 1957, Greta Garbo wanted to know how Fonda and I ever got together.

'Where did you meet? How did it happen?' she asked on that first visit. We were all sipping Bloody Marys, mine in those days all tomato juice with only a tiny dash of vodka.

'I don't know,' I replied, as I always replied. 'It just happened.'

She shook her head, and when she realized that I wasn't going to say any more, she suggested we go swimming – in the sea, rather than the pool. I followed her down the steps that led to a small private beach and there she did something strange – she took off her robe and stood there in front of me, as naked as a new-born baby. I believe she did it just to see my reaction, though I'm not too sure. I'm also not sure what George Schlee was doing at that precise moment.

I think I passed the test – as least I didn't take any notice. Garbo dived into the sea and that was that. I sat on the steps and watched her swim. She was still smooth and lean, with skin like a beautiful alligator. She did long, overarm strokes and then relaxed and called out more questions in her deep, lovely voice.

'Do you like Hollywood?' she asked.

'I suppose it is all right in some ways.'

'What about the people?'

'I don't know.' I thought for a second. 'I prefer New York.'

'Well, that's understandable.'

Clearly, little else was.

I liked Greta Garbo and I think, in the end, the feeling was mutual. She hated to be fussed over or spoken to as if she was special – and I never did that with anyone. I am glad she liked me in her own peculiar way.

Apart from the many parties and dinners we attended, we went as a family on several excursions – once to see Picasso. We all stood there in his studio and watched him paint, the way you might watch Yehudi Menuhin play the violin. It was very odd. Fonda had arranged it – probably to give himself inspiration. In fact, his oil painting did improve, though I don't know that Picasso was the cause.

It is rather fascinating for me to look at the two Henry Fonda originals that now stand on a shelf in my little flat in Eaton Place. The first, from the early days of our romance, is a vase of flowers, a realistic still life with the blooms arranged symmetrically on a light background. The second, from the dying months of our marriage, is wild and impressionistic, a scattering of leaves and petals in bright colours on a background that is dark and murky. Both are very competent, but the second is far more interesting.

Young and impressionable though I should have been, I wasn't so overwhelmed when we watched Picasso at work. He just ordered his assistants around the studio, like a ringmaster at the circus. It was fun, but not that much fun.

More interesting was the trip we made over the Pyrenees to Pamplona, to see the annual running of the bulls on 7 July. It was absolute madness: crowds of tourists, the desperate search to find a hotel room. We managed to find accommodation, though not together, but in various *pensiones* all over the city. We met the following morning. Jane and her boyfriend, James Franciscus, Peter's friends, Fonda and I. I clutched Fonda by one arm and Jane hung on the other.

'Afdera, you're not wearing any lipstick,' she said. 'You look fantastic without it.'

'Do I?' I replied. I didn't, of course.

'Yes, it looks great.'

The next day, Jane, who had been wearing bright red lipstick, wasn't wearing any, and she *did* look fantastic. The chameleon looks best in its natural colours. I wear make-up just so that I have something to do with my hands: you can take a compact from your bag, peer into the mirror and do a quick repair job. It's not vanity so much as a disguise for nervousness.

So, off we set to watch the running of the bulls.

'I haven't seen Peter,' Fonda said.

'He'll be here somewhere,' Jane answered. 'He wouldn't miss this for anything.'

We hurried along with the crowd and eventually we found ourselves a spot on one of the terraces above the street. We could hear a rumbling noise growing in the distance, the sound of hooves drumming on the cobblestones like an army on the march.

'I wish I could see Peter,' Fonda said again. He needn't have worried. Peter was there, for once, right in the centre of it all.

When the bulls begin the stampede, the young men who want to be matadors set off in front of them, running as fast as they can through the narrow passages that lead to the bullring. The unlucky are gored and trampled, some give up and cling to the terraces, and the best of them make it all the way. The front runners had just turned the corner and whom did we see there with his fair hair and long legs but Peter, speeding along with the best of them.

'There's not much he doesn't get up to,' Fonda said. He wasn't sure whether to be proud or ashamed.

The bulls passed, Peter lived to tell the tale, and that was that.

It was on this journey that I got to know James Franciscus a little better and, when I knew him, I realized he would never last with Jane. He was too nice and far too straightforward. Jane's personality was complex and, while it was still surfacing, I knew she would soon discard a man who was easy-going for others with a web of complications. They were on their way: a Greek bisexual her father despised, feminist friends, anti-war campaigners. Jane was continually changing shape and colour, blending into the background until she emerged looking for all the world as if she had invented the latest fad. She learned quickly and moved on just as quickly. It was only a few years later that she met Roger Vadim, and with him she sparkled: she became the sex symbol for which, despite all her changes, she is best remembered.

Before they married, Jane and Vadim came to visit me in New York –

she was dying for me to meet him and dying for me to give my opinion.
It was very sweet.

He appeared: dark hair, dark eyes that focused like a pair of spotlights,
his face lean and determined, and his movements as quick and as cunning
as those of a fox.

'Ah,' he said, opening his arms as he entered the door. 'So you are
the famous Afdera. I've heard so much about you.'

'Really? And what have you heard?'

He thought for a moment and then spoke in French.

'*Rien que les choses les plus merveilleuses. Dans votre propre univers
vous êtes le soleil.*'

'*Merci.*'

'*Et vous êtes ravissante, comme on me l'a toujours affirmé, et c'est
tout à fait vrai.*'

We laughed. Jane looked from face to face. Vadim was charming and
he didn't mean a word he said. He started up again, still speaking in
French, and said all the things a man might say to charm a woman. It
was most amusing, and I didn't mind at all. When that was over, he sat
on the sofa with Jane and they couldn't keep their hands off each other.
They kept touching and kissing. They did everything in front of me
except make love. At the time, they were preparing the film *Barbarella*,
so I suppose every spare moment was useful for Jane to get into the
part. It is strange how a woman's features change depending on the
man she is with. Jane's face was never particularly interesting, but with
Roger Vadim, instead of appearing American and healthy, she was
glowing and sensuous. If Vadim was the Svengali he was made out to
be, it was just what Jane needed.

I sat and watched them. With all the necking they did in public, I
couldn't help wondering what went on in the bedroom. Jane was acting
as if sex had just been discovered, although, in fairness, that may only
have been a projection of my own thoughts. At the time, I was finding
a new world within myself, a dimension Henry Fonda glimpsed like a
sailor from the deck of a ship, but a country that, together, we never
fully explored. I would explore it, but with others, not my husband.

The only other trip I made that summer of 1957 was alone and to
Venice. My mother was taken into hospital and, after I received a
telephone call from Lorian, I decided that my place was with the family.

Simba's death had pained Mama deeply and, although she had nothing against Fonda, she would have been more content had I married someone, if not closer to my own age, at least someone from my own background.

Carrying this perpetual sadness about her, Mama had recently made a pilgrimage to Lourdes, where she prayed for a miracle, a release from life. She was a devout Catholic and would never have considered committing suicide. Mama knew that her mind was going, but in her lucid moments she was very lucid.

I went to Venice by train and was taken to the hospital by motor launch. It was early evening, dusk was falling and a faint hint of mist clung to the canals. I stepped ashore and, though it was still summer, I shivered. The atmosphere was eerie. The Ca d'Oro was right opposite, like a gilded palace floating in the clouds; I could smell the fish from the market at the Rialto and, as soon as I turned towards the hospital building, I saw my mother through the window, so small and shrunken, like a little bird fading into the twilight. I didn't feel sad, I felt very alone. I was on the outside, peering in at the dancing shadows of life and death. I was engulfed by the mist, swallowed in the sound of the water that drummed against the wooden jetty. I felt as if I was standing at a crossroads, the arrows and destinations all hazy in the gloom.

I found Lorian waiting for me at Mama's bedside. Mama was sleeping. She seemed peaceful, more peaceful than ever. The operation had been to remove a growth and a part of her insides. It had been successful, but she had terminal cancer and was given only a short time to live. I glanced at my sister, but didn't speak. She looked me up and down, the way she always looked me up and down. I was immaculately dressed, tanned, my hair had been done.

'I see you're becoming more Americanized,' Lorian finally said.

'I could see all your little wheels turning round,' I replied. 'I knew you would have to say something.'

'Don't be so quick to take offence.'

'I'm not taking offence,' I retorted. 'Anyway, there's nothing wrong with looking Americanized. American women are usually very smart – smarter than some European women I know.'

'Really.'

It passed, as catty and unnecessary as always.

When a nurse came to give Mama her medication, Lorian and I

stepped outside and, for some reason still unknown to me, a young doctor took us to a room that contained a large refrigerator and showed us the parts that had been removed from our mother. I was more shocked than upset and, typically, I expressed my confused feelings in the wrong way.

'It's hard to believe that's where we both come from,' I muttered.

'What a strange person you are,' Lorian answered. She looked me up and down again, as if she might have missed something the last time.

'I didn't mean it like that.'

'The last thing we need is you and your cynical humour,' my sister broke in. She then changed the subject and asked: 'How long do you intend staying?'

'I don't know. While I'm needed, I'll stay,' I replied.

'Well, I'll be here. We don't want too many people, it will only upset her.'

'Yes, I suppose so.'

Lorian was really quite amazing. She was always plotting and always looking for new sources of funds for her husband. Lollo had dreams of becoming the leading light in the Fascist Party; he was given some ancient and obscure title in Rome – but though he invested a fortune in promoting himself, he never seemed to get very far.

Lorian's behaviour, though inexcusable, was at least understandable. She was like the Godfather and everything she ever did was for the family – for Lollo and her children. That banished any feelings of guilt she may have had, although those feelings had little chance of surfacing through the much deeper, darker resentment she had for me. I had not been a beautiful child, I wasn't particularly clever, but for some reason I was and had always been Mama's favourite.

It is all water under the bridge. I gave it no thought then, and now it is all history. It was only Mama who mattered. She came out of hospital and returned home to convalesce. She would live for just over another year and through that time, though the cancer cells multiplied, never once was she in pain. It may have been that the miracle she had prayed for had been granted, but I never saw it that way. When she died, I blamed myself for not being closer to her and giving her more comfort. And why, I wondered, had God allowed her to suffer so much when she had always been such a strong believer in him? She deserved a more peaceful death.

These feelings have faded, although they will never completely pass, because, paradoxically, I will never fully let go of my vague attachments to the church. Religion was so much a part of my family and the life of the community, it was taken for granted; it was simply there, like the sun in the sky. Now, if I feel like walking into a church and sitting down quietly, I do so. If it turns out to be a mosque, or a synagogue, or a Buddhist temple, it does just as well. Labels aren't important.

I had a lot of conflicting thoughts when I left Mama in San Trovaso. She was healing quickly and was in good spirits.

'Look after yourself,' she told me. 'And try to be happy.'

'Of course, Mama, I always do.'

'I hope so,' she said. 'That's all there is, you know.'

Her words remained in my mind as I watched the chauffeur load the luggage into the car. My mood was both gay and melancholy. In Venice I seemed to see everything through new eyes. It was all so ancient and so very beautiful, a fading, crumbling beauty selling itself to the tourist mob. But somehow that made no difference. Behind the bright colours and the gaudy signs that littered the Grand Canal, the proud buildings had the same quality as always. It was my city and I loved it. I loved every time-worn stone and swaying bridge and every plump pigeon that strutted through the Piazza San Marco. All were a part of me. My past was there, there in the mist that lay over the lagoon, and I knew instinctively that whatever happened, it was to Venice that I would always return.

The train pulled out of the main station, climbing over the hills of the Veneto, through fields all golden and ripening with crops, on to Milan and then south, the sun growing hotter as we reached the scorched Riviera coastline. I was glad to be on my own and have some time to rearrange my thoughts, which made me both subdued and completely unprepared for the welcome I received when I reached the villa.

Everyone was wearing clown-sized smiles and stretched out hugging arms from every direction. I had been away for twice as long as everyone had expected and even Peter and his friends appeared happy that I was back. They had all decided to hate me, *en bloc*, but they enjoyed the things that happened around me. As for Jane, she usually just watched and didn't say very much, but that day she was bubbling over.

'I'm so glad you're back, Afdera, so glad,' she said warmly.

Fonda pulled me to his side. 'It's been like a morgue here,' he stated.

'We didn't know what to do with ourselves.'

'For two days it was a relief to be quiet,' Jane added. 'On the third day the place seemed empty – and on the fourth, we really missed you ...'

When Jane was sweet, she was very, very sweet.

5 . Primi Pasticci

To be a part of Venice is to be a part of something that is wonderfully unique; somehow I have always felt that our destinies, as well as our fortunes, were oddly linked.

For hundreds of years it was one of the most powerful cities in the world and the main market place in Europe for all the exotic things that journeyed by sea from Arabia, India and the Orient. The merchants, the Franchettis among them, became wealthy and that wealth could be seen like a tapestry over the horizon: tall, elegant towers, gleaming domes, the varying architecture of Byzantine, Gothic and Renaissance palaces. An intricate web of canals joins more than one hundred small islands and all roads lead, like spokes to the hub of a wheel, to the breath-taking Piazza San Marco. Now it is a magnet to an endless stream of camera-armed tourists, while in the past it hosted bull fights, bear baiting, public celebrations and public executions. Three centuries ago, one unfortunate Franchetti who had seduced a priest was accused of being a witch and duly burnt to death in the centre of the square.

Venice was born from the scattered remains of the Roman empire. When the great cities of the mainland were sacked by the barbarians, the refugees fled to the remote islands, and there they laid the foundations of a city that was virtually impregnable. It was protected, not by walls, but by the shallow tidal waters of the lagoon. Warships were unable to get through without becoming stranded on the mud flats, and thus Venice was left to a life of peace and growing prosperity.

When I was a child, I often went to stay with Grandmama Moceniga at the Palazzo Rocca, a tall, imposing building that stands on the edge of the Grand Canal. My own home was in the country and, as I was used to spending my days in the fresh air, in Venice I did the same. Around the palace there is a small garden, statues peer out from behind bushes and trees, narrow pathways criss-cross the flower beds, and looming up beyond them are the high stone walls which even at an early age I found restricting. I needed space, lots and lots of space, and, as soon as I was able to open the gate, I stole out into the big wide world – and drove the poor governess of the time completely mad.

One of the things I quickly learned was that with my mother so generous and my family so well known, my credit was good. I could go into any shop and get whatever I wanted – candy bars, hair slides and ribbons, tiny gifts. How the bills were eventually paid and who paid them, I never knew. This was wonderful, of course, although it had the disadvantage of making me flippant and wasteful with money, usually other people's money. I was born, not with a silver spoon, but with a golden American Express card between my lips.

Fortunately, the Palazzo Rocca is unchanged. It is one of the few old palaces that hasn't been converted into a bank or a honeycomb of apartments and, no doubt for this reason, it was the one private home visited by Prince Charles and Princess Diana during their recent tour of Venice. My mother's brother, Uncle Giulio, and Nana, his wife, were so thrilled, it was still the main topic of conversation when I saw them months later.

Nana was exactly the same as I remembered her from my childhood. She is one of my favourite people, a gentlewoman in the traditional sense, yet someone with a keen mind and an equally keen interest in art, culture and politics. She also seems to have a great understanding of people. The servants at the palace all adore her and have been with her for generations – the complete opposite of her neighbour across the canal, my sister-in-law Kristina. What it comes down to is class, an innate nobility that has nothing to do with titles or lineage. Nana is a woman of quality and you can see it in her features, her neat grey hair, her kind yet intelligent eyes. When you are with her, you have the feeling of being with someone who is special. She is a woman who could have done anything, but had devoted her life to her husband. Uncle Giulio, who wasn't a Fascist, was interned in a German prison camp during the war, an experience from which he never fully recovered.

During my last visit, we were leafing through the royal snapshots when suddenly Nana stopped and gave me a worried look.

'Afdera, I haven't offered you anything to eat,' she said.

'That's all right, I've just eaten.'

'Are you sure now?' Nana said more sternly. 'You are eating properly?'

'Yes, of course I am,' I replied. 'I eat like a horse.'

'That certainly is a change. When you were a child you would go all day without eating and then empty the larder in the middle of the night.' She laughed. 'The thing was, you still didn't eat very much – the maid used to find everything stored under the bed.'

'Including lots of nutshells?'

'Yes,' she answered. 'Including lots of nutshells.'

We finished looking at the photographs, drank coffee and, as I was leaving, my aunt pushed a very large lire note into my hand. There was no way of saying no. To Nana, I am still the naughty little girl I always was.

As childhood passed and I became a teenager, I still crept out of the Palazzo Rocca, only then it was at night, not during the day. I was discovering life and learning about myself and somehow I knew that, in order to do that, it was necessary to do just about everything Nana had strictly forbidden.

It was the same as going through all the books in the library that my mother had barred me from reading: I always did what was forbidden and I was always caught. For a long time, I thought that was just the nature of things, and it came as a complete shock when I found out that my big sister Lorian had a vast network of spies. Even without them, Venice was that sort of place. Everyone knew what everyone else was doing. It was cut off, an island made remote by the quivering curtains of mist and timeless by the lack of motor cars and noise.

'*From the very beginning, Venice recognized itself as a strange and mysterious creation.*' They are the words of the Swiss historian Jacob Burckhardt, words that I couldn't help thinking were also written for me. I loved it and I loved to be out in the middle of it all; and this, for some reason, was a continual thorn in Lorian's paw. She was the one who should have been named Simba.

'She's starting too early,' she would tell Mama. 'You know we are going to have trouble.'

Poor Mama. She hated scenes as much as Lorian thrived on them and, once started, Lorian would charge on like a crazed bull in the bullring. The word 'trouble' was usually followed by an ominous pause. Mama would look anxious and then Lorian would add in an outraged voice:

'We are going to have trouble with *sex*.'

At the mention of the word, Mama would close up completely.

'Leave her alone, Lorian,' she would say. 'I'm sure she will be all right.'

'I'm only thinking of Afdera,' Lorian would add righteously. 'It's her future I'm worried about.'

It was hard to know if my sister spoke from genuine concern or her own experience. I would be shuffling my feet, Mama would be embarrassed and Simba would look forlorn.

'Afdera,' she would say in her soft, faraway voice, 'do try to be good.'

That always floored me. Simba said less than anyone else, which meant that when she did say something, I couldn't help but take notice.

'Yes, I will. I'm sorry. I won't do it again.' Whatever it was, I was always promising 'not to do it again'.

In some ways, the division between my sisters and me was simply the generation gap. Lorian and Simba were young women during the war, and did their growing up in that historical black hole between the wars. Everything that belonged to that era had faded and blown away like the leaves in autumn, and the spring was bringing in something new and wonderful. Things were changing and especially in Venice.

Mussolini's controversial causeway linking the islands to the mainland was completed in 1931, just before I was born, and, as if it had been built just for me, or as if our destinies were truly entwined, while it brought the world to Venice it was a bridge that would take me into the world. Like a kite string or an umbilical cord, it would also draw me back.

As 1950 rolled into view, I was a teenager and, with the self-confidence of youth and the optimism of a new decade, I knew deep down in my very bones that I was to be a part of the future: concepts, morals, fashions and everything were evolving into something that those on the wrong side of that generation gap would never recognize. It was all beginning, and I didn't have long to wait. People like Hemingway, John Huston, Lennie Bernstein, Elsa Maxwell and many others were friends of mine long before I sat down to dine with Henry Fonda. Venice was a village and you couldn't help but bump into everyone who passed through, so it was natural that when somebody was there I was introduced.

I met people at the annual film festival, at the theatre, Harry's

Bar, the fashionable cafés – everywhere but at the house of Peggy Guggenheim – and even *I* didn't go there. To enter was to abandon all hope, as if it was Dante's Inferno. It was infamous, a legend, a low white building that stood between two Gothic palaces on the Grand Canal, as if the gleaming façade outside was camouflage for all the dark, diabolic happenings that went on inside. Trees grew from the roof, weird music poured from the windows and the parties were imagined to be wild orgies with drugs and nudity.

Peggy Guggenheim was at one time married to the painter Max Ernst and he and his Surrealist friends were rumoured not only to prey on innocent young Venetian girls, but actually to consort with homosexuals. The very thought took my breath away. I knew what it meant, although I wasn't sure what it entailed.

Mama had given us all complexes because of her attitude towards sex. She had scolded me so forcefully when I kissed her on the lips that when a boy got round to kissing me, it came as a great shock. We were skiing at Cortina; I fell; he pulled me into his arms and the kiss was marvellous.

When I did finally abandon all hope and enter one of those famous parties, it was another big let-down. Nobody had two heads, nobody was naked, and the homosexuals were the same as all the other men: they just wore better shoes. As for Peggy Guggenheim, she was an extraordinary woman, who married five times, served as a magnet for young artists and writers and had one of the best collections of paintings in the world – a collection that is still in Venice and on show at the Guggenheim Gallery.

That was reality. During the time when I was still awed by the myth, an evening came when I was passing the house in a motor boat and I looked up and saw the most peculiar figure lying full-length across one of the windows. The lights were behind and in silhouette I could see an enormous head and the stunted body of a dwarf. The boat moved on and I thought no more about it until the next day, when the same figure appeared on the dock outside Harry's Bar, not a dwarf exactly, but very tiny. He was all in white with a straw hat, like some exotic sea creature that had just been washed up by the tide. As it happened, I had just read the amazing book *Other Voices, Other Rooms*. His name was on everyone's lips. I had seen the photographs in the press and now I recognized Truman Capote. Several years later, when I was married and living in New York, it was inevitable that Capote and I would meet again. When we did, I broke my own golden rule and made a point of introducing myself.

'I saw you a long time ago in Venice,' I then said. 'At Peggy Guggenheim's.'

'Wasn't she a darling?' he replied. 'I suppose we were all high on something?'

'Yes, I suppose we were.'

I didn't mention that I had seen him from *outside* the Guggenheim establishment, and he didn't say that he didn't remember me. I think he was rather proud of his memory and, while he was sorting it through, we both just stood there. I was a head taller; Truman was peering up from the shade of a Toulouse-Lautrec hat that framed his large head. There was a smile on the corners of his lips, but his eyes were otherwise engaged. They were dark and knowing and they were moving over my features as if he intended painting my portrait.

When the study was over he said: 'How does it feel to be the new Mrs Fonda?'

'It's all right,' I replied. 'He's a lovely man.'

He thought about that for a moment. 'Any woman who calls her husband a lovely man has got to have a mind of her own,' he told me. 'Perhaps you're just what he needs.'

'I didn't know that he needed anything.'

'We all need something,' he said sharply. 'And Fonda needs to learn how to be generous.'

'He is generous.'

He laughed. 'He's a mean bastard,' he retorted. 'And you look like the kind of woman who's going to take him for everything he's got.'

I think he wanted to be controversial, or even upset me, but he didn't upset me at all. I thought he was fabulous. We clicked, although neither of us knew why. I wasn't an intellectual – and he liked intellectuals; he wasn't tall and dashing – and, at the time, I liked men who were tall and dashing. There was simply something that neither of us ever understood, so we just enjoyed each other and didn't discuss it.

Truman had a high, whiny voice and an uncanny way of summing people up in a very few words. He found their weak spot and then stabbed it with his finger. With those he despised, his comments were like sabre slashes. The wealthy socialites of New York drew him into their bosom, knowing all the time that they were fondling a viper. He was like the court jester in traditional Italian theatre; he made a fool of himself, only to make bigger fools of the king and his courtiers. His perception enabled him to see the good and the bad in people at the same time. Fonda was stingy, although in fact with me he wasn't – and I could have 'taken Fonda for everything', though when it came to it I didn't. If I had been a real schemer there would have been four Mrs Fondas, not five, and I would have been the rich widow.

So Truman Capote was wrong, but he had recognized a certain potential. He once described Jane Fonda as a fake and, when he was asked years later if he thought she'd had a genuine change of values, he replied: 'She's had a genuine change of bank accounts.'

He was quick, clever, straight to the point, and he was forever in the centre of something: a libel action, a drama and, at parties, a group of beautiful women – Jackie Kennedy and Lee Radziwill, Lillian Hellman, whom he adored, and Babe Paley, a woman who looked like Kay Kendall, but was very different. She was one of those rare people who could combine being both an intellectual and a marvellous wife and hostess.

During that period, I rarely saw Capote with a man, except his companion, another gnome, a little mouse who never said a word. By then, of course, I knew a bit more about homosexuals and had discovered that they tended to like certain men who weren't homosexuals. It goes without saying that my husband wasn't one of them, although he had a penchant for, as he put it, 'rescuing lesbians'. He had nothing against people who happened to be gay. He just didn't like Truman Capote.

'I don't know what you see in that evil little thing,' he said.

'Only that he's a genius,' I answered.

'The only thing he has a genius for is getting on my nerves.'

It was lovely to see Fonda worked up about something. Usually when we disagreed, his blue eyes would fill with clouds, his face would turn to stone and his lips would remain sealed. Once only he lashed out and hit me, but then he collapsed in a fit of tearful remorse.

'Look what you're doing to me,' he wept. 'Look what you've made me do.'

It was actually just the slightest of slaps and I didn't worry about it at all. If he had done it more often, I would have respected him more and then, who knows what the future might have held?

And so, with the bad chemistry that existed between my husband and the little genius, coupled with the fact that I wasn't the sort of person to be a satellite in orbit around someone else, Capote and I only met when our paths happened to cross. On one occasion, we were both spending the weekend with mutual friends in a country house in New England. I had just got out of the bath and while I was drying myself Capote waltzed in without knocking. I wasn't wearing a stitch. Capote didn't give me so much as a second glance, but went straight for the small army of tubes and bottles and jars that lined the shelf.

'Darling,' he said. 'We use all the same creams.'

'Great minds?'

'No, no, my dear, great bodies,' he replied. He paused for a moment and then turned round. 'Afdera,' he stressed in a hurt voice, 'you don't think I didn't notice?'

Red roses coloured my cheeks. He sat on the edge of the tub and watched me dress the way you might watch a child tying its shoelaces and then we went down to the drawing room to have a drink. We had cocktails which he claimed were made from a secret family recipe, though he probably just made it up as he went along. He was in one of those moods.

Later that evening and in a very different mood he said: 'You know something, you may not make Fonda happy and you may not be the ideal wife, but you've got plenty of intuition.'

'Why, thank you,' I replied. With Truman you couldn't help but talk with a Southern accent.

'I mean it,' he whined. 'You're not as frivolous as you make out.'

I peered at him through my dark glasses and didn't say another word. I felt naked again. Talking to Capote, the Capote inside the court jester, was like talking to yourself in the mirror. You saw yourself, not as other saw you, but as you really were. He was a man who always made me laugh and, though he joined in, you had the feeling that he wasn't really laughing at all. You could see the conflict in his eyes, penetrating and questioning, childlike, sometimes sad and distant. He was trapped in a misshapen, stunted body, when inside was the tall, beautiful woman he wanted to be.

With most of his comments I agreed, though not every time, and particularly not with his views on Jane Fonda. For all her disguises, Jane was always the same get-up-and-go creature working to reach the top of each new mountain, and she didn't give up until she reached the top. If she doesn't think a lot of me and people like me, it's hardly surprising – though it doesn't mean that I don't have every respect for her. Ambition just isn't in my nature. I enjoy *not* having goals and *not* having to get up in the morning. Each achievement is just another enslavement that drives you on to achieve the next thing – and I could never see the point in that.

One other small thing Truman Capote and I disagreed on was Venice. He once said it was like eating a whole box of chocolate liqueurs all in one go – far too sweet and sickly. For me, Venice is a Christmas tree laden with the most wonderful gifts.

6 . Beautiful Creatures

New York has such an extraordinary adrenalin it's like having a shot of B12 in the arm just being there. In London I feel protected, as if life is going on behind a glass wall, and, for the present, that is what I want. I am lucky. I have a nice flat and a nice circle of friends, new ones as well as those who date all the way back to the Big Apple. Life is *reasonably* happy and I am *reasonably* content; but when I fly across the Atlantic and arrive in New York, I feel a nostalgia as sharp as a toothache. I close my eyes and the vision that rolls before my eyelids is an amazing movie that has yet to be shot, a movie made up of tiny memories like pinpricks and endless amusing cameos with me, not as the heroine, but as one of the players in some wonderful, incredible game.

I always seem to arrive in the evening, always well gone on something. I have two porters, too much luggage. The customs and immigration men are all young, with fresh faces and short-sleeved shirts. Everyone is in a mad rush and the energy creates a buzz you just have to tune into. If you don't feel the buzz, you don't like New York.

My suitcases are loaded into a car, and soon after I leave the airport I pass under a bridge, crest a hill and then I see all the lights of the Manhattan skyscrapers. That's when I really start to get high. The air smells invigorating, as if it has been wandering through the most interesting places, and the sky has a pink tinge, even when it's snowing. For years and years I used to look at the lights and imagine that one of them belonged to me and that, inside it, I was having a ball.

To do that, of course, you need people. Once upon a time, everyone who was there had a very special energy, a quality. There was nothing crummy or phoney about anyone. If they were gangsters, they were proper gangsters. The artists were artists and the chic were well dressed, well spoken, well informed and civilized. It is awful to be such a snob, but they were called the beautiful people because they *were* beautiful people. Everything that was mediocre and in-between came later with those who were cashing in on the peddlers, the pushers, the second-rate. Café society became Nescafé society and a tiny fragment of something that was quite perfect began to tarnish, to rust and then to disappear.

It had needed very special circumstances for this world to exist: the prosperity of the late fifties without the mass advertising, packaging, promoting, mass communications of the mid-sixties. It was all as quick and concentrated as the blink of an eye – the few years between 1957 and 1965 – and it was then, by sheer coincidence, that I had my home in New York, first on 74th Street when I was married to Henry Fonda and then, later, my own apartment on Park Avenue.

I'm not a big walker, but on the days when Fonda was rehearsing, I would walk and walk and walk. We were living on 74th and Lexington and in that neighbourhood lots of small shops were opening – Bamboo, Little England, Serendipity, Azuma. It was a pleasure just to window shop, although as Hank had given me a wallet filled with plastic cards I usually did more than that. For some reason I never had any money, cash money, which did cause problems when I wanted to get a taxi or buy something in secret; particularly when I wanted to buy something in secret.

Another area where I liked to walk was Greenwich Village, with its noisy bars and cafés, live shows and people who looked ghastly during the hours of daylight. There were Chinese shops selling the oddest things and there was one Chinese restaurant where you had to sit at an immense table in the kitchen and eat with the cooks and waiters. It was filthy and I loved it. I could hear the sound of guitars and folk songs drifting from the windows at the Chelsea Hotel and on the sidewalk were the colourfully-dressed composers, some destined for great fame and even greater fortunes. One group I got to know rather well was the trio Peter, Paul and Mary, whom I first met through the Italian journalist Furio Colombo in the days when Mary was washing dishes by day and singing at night. She had a little boy whom she sometimes left at our house with Fidalma and who played with Amy when she was staying. That was also Bob Dylan's era, although I didn't discover him until much later – on the stereo.

While Truman Capote had introduced me to a few outlandish scenes in the village, so too did Furio Colombo, who, with his newsman's nose, somehow found out what was going on long before anyone else. I would sit in dark corners and consume strange dishes. The conversation sparkled and the air was invariably charged with something decidedly pungent. Marijuana was becoming very fashionable.

Furio Colombo was always a good friend – in fact, he was almost too good a friend. When Fonda's biography was published in 1981, his newspaper, *Corriere della Sera*, devoted half the front page to a photograph, not of Henry Fonda, but of me, with a long article by Furio that negated just about everything that had been said about me in the book. It was terribly sweet, although it then sparked off a controversy that I didn't really want. I actually didn't mind if the things were true or not and even found it rather amusing that some of the funnier incidents that happened with Fonda and me were attributed in his memoirs to Shirlee, the cute little Cinderella who became his last wife.

My annoyance over the book soon passed, as everything is forever passing, so quickly that we don't pause to take breath. I certainly didn't in 1957. I just enjoyed life. Elvis Presley was bursting from the radio day and night, a rage and an outrage; David Lean's *The Bridge on the River Kwai* won the Academy Award for the best film; and the Russians beat America to the post by putting their first sputnik and then the first monkey into space – all events debated hotly over dinner tables and in crowded rooms, without impinging on anyone's life. Everyone I knew was marching to the sound of his own drum and preparing his own projects – movies, masterpieces, exhibitions. My own was trying to work out how to get some money for Christmas.

The festival had arrived in no time at all. Jane was over from Paris, having stayed on to study art after the summer at Cap Ferrat; Peter and Amy appeared, and Fonda dressed a monstrous tree with lights and glitter. In America, they have Christmas in the morning, so we were all up hours earlier than was necessary and then had to sit there trying to be nice to each other while we opened our presents. It was terrifying. Women I had met twice at parties sent the most gorgeous things and I hadn't even thought of sending anything to them. Some of those kind ladies truly had hearts of gold, though later I realized that others sent gifts as much for good business as good will. Lots of the wives kept careful watch over their husbands' careers and, at the time, Henry Fonda was as well connected as I was thoroughly naïve.

Next came Hank's gift to me – something *really* extraordinary. I had been mumbling that I needed a hobby. I had decided that I wanted to be creative and artistic. I peeled off the wrapping paper and when I took it out of the case I couldn't believe my eyes: a *banjo*!

Hank was wearing a bright smile to match his bright new sweater. 'Look,' he said, pulling out an envelope. 'This comes with it.'

Inside the envelope was a receipt for twenty-five lessons. I was to begin learning immediately after Christmas.

I was speechless.

That banjo was to follow me for years – though I only saw my instructor on three occasions. He was a dwarf, a real dwarf, not like Truman Capote, with enormous feet and an enormous beard, just like the little Santa Claus that Fonda had stuck on top of the tree. He was also a tyrant. In those days, I used to wear my nails very long, like an eagle, and for the first lesson he made me cut half of them off. I couldn't have imagined a worse form of suffering. I spent the whole of the second lesson convincing the man that I didn't want to cut any more nails off and at the third, I gave him a large Scotch and said goodbye. I told him that I was going back to Italy and he seemed quite sad, although when I asked him for a refund on the remaining lessons he almost had a fit.

'You want a refund?' he screamed. 'You must be crazy. I've never been so insulted in all my life.'

I stared back in amazement. He was clenching his fists and gritting his teeth.

'I'll tell you something, lady,' he then said. 'You won't find a better banjo teacher in New York.'

At that, he stormed out of the door and I never saw him again.

My gift to Hank was also a great surprise. When we were in Toledo, he had taken a photograph of us both under the famous tree with the famous El Greco skyline in the background. He set the camera up with a delayed timer and jumped into the picture just as the shutter was opening. It was perfect: he looked boyishly pleased with himself and I looked shy and nice. Hank loved that photograph, so I gave it to an old friend of mine, Fulco della Verdura, an eccentric Italian duke who designed beautiful jewellery and painted the most exquisite miniatures. One I remember was of the Piazza San Marco, including the pigeons, and the whole thing is no bigger than a postage stamp.

The painting of Fonda and me was just as marvellous – but then I had the problem of paying Fulco and paying for everything else. I had worried about it for weeks, but then, on one of my walks, I discovered a pawn shop and it was there that I deposited my minks and pearls. Fonda, a week after Christmas, sent Giuseppe to get everything back, a task he had to perform many times in the future.

Fonda was thrilled with the Fulco miniature and it kept him happy for a long time. From then on I always gave him paintings and he began quite a good collection. I believed in finding new artists, although sometimes I would buy something by a known painter. The most expensive was a Morandi – heaven knows where I got the money for that! Fonda would occasionally mutter a few complaints about my trips to the pawnbroker, but in a way it was his own fault. He gave me plastic credit cards, but I never had a bank account and he had forbidden me to use the money from my allowance in Italy. That was piling up nicely.

As soon as the drama of Christmas was over, we had the drama of *Two for the Seesaw* to contend with. Hank had been in rehearsals solidly from the time we got back from the Riviera, but though lots of changes were made in the play, with each day that passed his doubts about it became more intense. It was the story of a Nebraska lawyer who goes to New York, where he has an affair with a much younger woman. Fonda played opposite the then unknown Anne Bancroft. Her part was rather moving and by far the larger, while his was awkward, ungratifying and appeared undemanding. Fonda's roles always seemed that way on stage and that was his skill.

'I've made the biggest mistake of my life doing this,' he kept saying (it had been the same with *Twelve Angry Men*), but he had signed the contract, so he went to work every day and gave a masterly performance when the play opened.

It was the night of 16 January 1958. It was raining and the crowds splashed across Broadway to the brightly-lit restaurants where their tables were waiting. Anne Bancroft had skipped off in the centre of her entourage of admirers and I dragged along with my husband, not to Sardi's, where we always went after his opening nights, but home to a quiet supper with a small group of Fonda intimates. Two of my friends, Rudi and Consuelo Crespi, were also there. They were the most sociable couple in the world and couldn't understand why there was a sudden gloom hanging over us. Actually, I couldn't either.

We sat as if for a funeral supper in Jack Peacock's Venetian dining-room, picked at a meal that Fidalma had prepared and waited for the morning papers. The first editions are on the streets shortly after midnight. Soon after, Fonda's press agent appeared with the whole bundle under his arm. He spread them out in front of Fonda and then eased himself out of sight behind his chair. No one uttered a sound as Fonda opened the pages and went very slowly and very carefully through the reviews. He read them out and, though there wasn't a single word of criticism for his performance, the praise for Anne Bancroft was so great it seemed to put him into the deepest shade. 'A New Star Shines over Broadway', 'Tonight a Star Is Born' – all the old favourites were there, and as Fonda let the words fall from his lips, his face grew longer and longer. Finally he said how happy he was for Anne Bancroft, which was nice, because he didn't find it easy to work with her.

The rest of us at the table remained quiet for a long time and then the others all started to say how unfair the critics were and how wonderful Hank had been. It didn't make a scrap of difference. I knew him and I knew he was suffering. It showed in his eyes: they were grey instead of blue. He was slipping into one of his tragic states and looked so sorry for himself, I felt like walking around the table and giving him a good hard shake. In fact, metaphorically speaking, that's just what I did do.

'Listen, Hank,' I said. 'I want a new coat.'

He glared back at me.

'It's a mink. It's a new colour and it's cut a new way,' I pressed.

Fonda shook his head without focusing on me and continued to read the reviews.

'Are you crazy?' a voice whispered. I think it was Rudi Crespi.

'Be quiet, can't you?' said someone else.

I didn't take any notice.

'Hank. It's winter. I want a new coat.'

Now, my husband closed his newspaper and looked at me with murder in his eyes.

'You are a spoilt bitch,' he said.

'I don't care. I want a new coat.'

'Don't you ever think about anything but yourself? Ever?'

'What's that supposed to mean?'

'Exactly what I said. You're a spoilt bitch.'

The others at the table were loving every minute of it, their heads turning from side to side, like the spectators at Wimbledon. They waited with breath held for a beat of two.

'Hank,' I then said in a quiet, controlled voice, 'what are you getting so worked up about? The play's going to be the biggest hit on Broadway. It's going to run for five years. They've all said how marvellous you are. A new star is born ... so what?' I paused for a moment. 'I want a new coat.'

The Crespis remained quiet. Everyone was cross with me, but Fonda finally squeezed out a tiny smile, a real one, and instead of going into one of his long depressions, he opened a bottle of Jack Daniels and we all got drunk.

By the time our guests managed to stagger home, the sun was about ready to begin a new day. We went to bed, but for Hank the moment of fatigue had passed. He had remained frustrated by the reviews and this, coupled with all the alcohol he didn't usually drink, made him into the most thoughtful and ingenious lover. It was a night to remember and, when I did finally close my eyes, I must have had a large smile on my lips.

'Why all the smiles?' Hank asked.

'I don't know,' I replied. 'I suppose it's because I'm so simple: I laugh when I'm happy and cry when I'm sad. No?'

I'm not sure that I meant that exactly and I don't know if my husband said anything else. I had fallen fast asleep.

Two weeks later, I was wearing a new coat.

That high energy, floating-in-the-air feeling I got from my very doorstep at East 74th Street didn't exist beneath the enduring blue skies of California. Fonda much preferred working on Broadway, but it was the movies that paid the bills, so it was to Hollywood we migrated for three months each year.

In New York I was a theatre widow. I would have lunch with someone, spend the early evening with friends and then meet Fonda after the curtain came down. It was like having my cake and eating it. I had three lives and the best of all worlds, though, naturally, this did cause a few problems. If I spent a lot of time with the same friend – a man – rumours that I was having a torrid affair would erupt as surely as Old Faithful in Yellowstone Park. It was never true. To me it was perfectly normal for a girl to have admirers and, for another thing, though the free love age was on its way, it hadn't quite arrived.

Life on the West Coast was completely different. There were long days with Fonda at the studios and me shopping or sitting beside somebody's pool and evenings filled with an endless round of dinners and galas – the men in formal black ties and the women in wonderful gowns, usually designed less to cover than to reveal – brown skin, a producer husband, something. Some of the women I knew worked hard at being placed on the 'best dressed' lists published in the magazines – even I was listed from time to time, although it always came as just as big a surprise to me as it did to everyone else.

The parties were often rather stuffy and so similar, few have lodged in my mind. One of the exceptions was the night our hosts employed the services of a gypsy lady who told fortunes. I knew my father had been interested in palms and the occult, an odd aspect of his personality, but I had never had the chance of having a reading. I was fascinated.

The large drawing-room where we first gathered was filled with people clinking glasses and making introductions. Hank wandered off somewhere with Gary Cooper, probably in the opposite direction from John Wayne, who was standing alone and gazing idly at the sea of faces. I turned away in case our eyes met, but, as if fate had willed it, I was suddenly talking to Mrs Wayne – Pilar, a Latin like myself, only from Peru.

'You know, your husband and my husband, they hate each other,' she whispered.

I knew exactly why. John Wayne had named various people as having Communist leanings during the McCarthy witch-hunts and Fonda had never forgotten it. I knew, but I didn't think Pilar did and it wasn't my place to inform her.

Instead I said: 'They're just like two children.'

'Yes,' she replied brightly. 'Like two schoolboys.'

We laughed and agreed on all sorts of things as we gradually circled the room and made our way to the fortune teller. She was in the adjoining room. We were about to enter when we were stopped by the beautiful Mrs Gregory Peck – Veronique, French, a former journalist and a lady with very definite opinions.

'I wonder why the fortune teller's here,' she said. 'We don't need these things – we have everything.'

She was probably right, but it was only a bit of fun.

Pilar and I had been joined by Merle Oberon, Anne (Mrs Kirk Douglas) and Rocky (Mrs Gary Cooper) and the four of us all hovered in the doorway like cartoon characters on the edge of a cliff. We were all holding our breath and glancing at each of the others in turn. We gave a group shrug and then plunged forward.

When it came to my turn with the gypsy, I held out my palm. The woman ran her forefinger over the various lines and then said one word: '*Clouds.*' She paused for an eternity and finally added in a dark voice: 'I see nothing but clouds.'

She went on and gave me lots of little warnings that I instantly forgot. I was only treating it as a game; I didn't know that some fortune tellers really do have an amazing and uncanny power. In those days I wasn't even aware of my own birth sign, which made it more delightful when I discovered some of the secrets of astrology. I'm Cancer – sensitive, creative, rather divine, but not always very good at listening!

All the men at the party pretended to be sceptical. Frank Sinatra, Kirk Douglas and Gregory Peck had stopped outside the door. Mr Peck had agreed with every word that came out of his wife's mouth. I chose that moment to say something that she disagreed with and Kirk Douglas responded by pointing his chin at me like an accusing finger.

'You're just a pain in the arse,' he said.

I bristled, but didn't take a lot of notice. Kirk Douglas obviously disliked me on sight and was not about to change his mind. He was one of those men who believed that a wife's place was carrying her husband's name like a banner to the various charity groups she organized with other wives. Not all, but certainly a large number of those women were content to be a Mrs Something-or-Other. I wasn't one of them. I was happy to be married to Hank, but the thought of dissolving myself into his persona had never occurred to me. For that matter, it had never occurred to him either.

It was some time after that party that I met Kirk Douglas for the second time. He was making a film in Death Valley with Peter Ustinov and I had gone on the trip with Peter and his wife Suzanne, while Fonda was busy on another project. I loved it – the dry heat and a pure white space that goes on forever, sitting over the desert like an aura.

I can't remember the circumstances, but one afternoon, I found myself cornered.

'You know something, you're not such a pain in the arse after all,' Kirk Douglas said. Then he did something I still can't believe could have happened. He pinched me, *where* goes without saying, and in a way that I found most surprising. I was no longer a teenager and he wasn't Ernest Hemingway. Kirk Douglas was very sure of himself and not exactly modest. I thought him bizarre.

From Death Valley, we went one evening to Las Vegas. The small plane flew so low to the ground I could see the individual rocks of the desert, which made me even more terrified than usual. Hank wasn't there, but he had telephoned and warned my companions that I was likely to become hysterical on the flight. I did – and they were still ashamed of me.

It passed. We arrived and went to watch Sinatra singing at the Sands. Afterwards, at the casino, Dean Martin, who had started life as a croupier, took over the dealer's job at the blackjack table. He moved the cards through his hands and I watched spellbound. His fingers were so delicate and dextrous – so strange-looking I just had to reach out and touch one.

'They're all real, Afdera,' Dean said. I thought he was marvellous, really *simpatico*; I liked him a lot.

Another memorable night in California was a party to 'launch' me at the home of Bill and Edith Goetz. He was one of the great producers of the time and she was the sister of Irene Selznick and daughter of the legendary Louis B. Mayer, the head of Metro-Goldwyn-Mayer throughout the golden age of Hollywood. Mayer had died the previous year, in 1957, and it was still being said that the only reason so many people went to his funeral was that they all wanted to make sure that he was really dead. L. B. Mayer was like a Rajah and had been universally loved, hated, feared and respected.

The Goetz home was a monument to that age. It was in Beverly Hills, a fine, spacious mansion with Roman columns decorating the main façade in a style that made me think immediately of the Villa Franchetti. Inside, it was completely different and far more spectacular. The hallway was filled with paintings by the Impressionists – Picasso from his blue period and his pink period, Monet, Édouard Manet, Renoir – including the lady with the straw hat that before I had only seen on postcards. It was truly amazing.

I stared at the walls as if I was in a gallery and, as I ambled into the living-room, I almost fell over the actress and dancer Juliet Prowse. We both laughed and, from the sublime to the mundane, we both forgot about the masterpieces and talked about ourselves. That night, she had come with Frank Sinatra. They were very close and he was on top of the world, which made a nice change. For me, Sinatra was a puzzle: for all the broads and for all the people who crowded around him, he often seemed a particularly solitary and lonely man.

As for Juliet, she was absolutely stunning. She was wearing white satin trousers and had legs that were so long and slender, I couldn't help asking her how she managed to stay so slim.

'I dance,' she said. 'I dance for hours every single day.'

We began talking about make-up. Mrs Danny Kaye and Merle Oberon – a lady who really did take me under her wing – passed through and we all said hello. Then Juliet advised me to wear lipstick that was less harsh, she suggested that I pluck my eyebrows and finally said how comfortable she felt wearing trousers.

'You should try them.'

'I'm not really a trousers person,' I said.

'Of course you are,' she laughed. 'You only have to be slim and you're slim . . . how do *you* do it?'

'I don't know,' I answered. 'I don't do anything.'

And it was true, I didn't take any exercise – a stroll around the stores, the occasional dip in the pool and, in the winter, skiing and sometimes ice skating – I had learnt to skate as a child and wasn't too bad at it. At dinner parties I ate whatever was put in front of me and if I didn't get fat, it must have been that I was worried about something, though I can't think what.

In many ways I was fortunate to arrive in Hollywood when I did. I felt comfortable being one of the young ones with the older, establishment figures. I would never have felt right as a hippy, jogger, health-food enthusiast or any of the other types that appeared a few years later. With these fads seemed to come an even greater narcissistic fascination with the body that to me was really rather silly. After talking to Juliet Prowse, I did lighten my lipstick, but I never plucked my eyebrows – they only grew again. I felt it was the first step to cosmetic surgery – breast lifts, face lifts. Gary Cooper would eventually have the bags under his eyes removed, which made me very sad. I actually like to see men with bags under their eyes. Changing your outlook is one thing, probably a good thing – your face and form is quite another.

But such thoughts belonged to the future – after I had fallen in love with a man who wasn't tall, handsome or well known – and back in the Goetz living-room I was busy shaking hands with this one and that one, the familiar faces smiling down at me from famous shoulders, as well as from the walls. The Impressionists were everywhere.

When we all trooped into the long dining-room to eat, I found myself next to a man who stared at me as if I was a giant ice cream, or a great movie star he adored. It was very embarrassing. It went on for so long I thought his eyes were going to pop out and land in the soup. But, finally, he sat back in his chair, vigorously shaking his head.

'Well?' I had to ask.

'You're Clea,' he said.

'What,' I replied. 'Clea who?'

'Clea ... from Alexandria.'

'Oh, no I'm not.'

'Oh, yes you are.'

Then it dawned on me: Clea from *The Alexandria Quartet*. Lawrence Durrell's set of four books had just been published.

'Ah,' I said, 'I'm certainly not.'

He smiled. 'You've read them, then?'

'I've read one of them,' I answered. 'And I'm not Clea.'

'I think you are.'

I shrugged. 'Who are you?' I then asked.

He lowered his voice to a whisper and said darkly: 'I'm Adrian.'

'Oh,' I said, none the wiser.

I discovered later that Adrian was a dress designer married to the actress Janet Gaynor – Hank's companion further along the table. They were chatting away as if they had known each other forever, which they had. Way, way back in 1935, Janet had played opposite Hank in *The Farmer Takes A Wife* – his first film in Hollywood and, as a play, his first major role on Broadway. It was the foundation stone upon which Fonda's career was to grow and, though he then went from one triumph to the next, that early success had remained a sweet memory. Fonda could be cold and hard, but he was also soft and sentimental.

The Stewarts were also present that night and it was with my divine friend Gloria Stewart that I made my way after dinner to another room filled with paintings. I recognized a little-known Fantin-Latour and, when I said so, everyone was most impressed and thought I knew more than I really did.

Jimmy Stewart was right behind me.

'I didn't know you were a connoisseur,' he said.

'I don't think I am,' I answered.

Hank looked very satisfied. He always did when I surprised people.

We were all made to sit down. One set of lights dimmed and, as they did so, the floor at the other end of the room rose up and seated there were all the members of the staff – chefs, under-chefs, maids. I was still startled by this when suddenly, right before my eyes, all the Picassos and Renoirs vanished into thin air and the wall became a blank white screen. The rest of the lights dimmed, a projector spun into life and, as I sat back in a mild state of shock, the credits for a brand new film began to roll. It was *Sayonara*, made by Bill Goetz and starring Marlon Brando, who mumbled in the most peculiar accent from beginning to end.

The thing that was nice about watching the film was that all the guests remained in one group. Usually, the men disappeared with their cigars and brandy and the women fluttered together like a flock of chattering seagulls – the chatter invariably about children and the problems they had finding help. Neither affected me. I didn't have any children – I like children, but I have never longed to have any of my own – and my couple, Fidalma and Giuseppe, went with us everywhere.

Once more I had the best of all possible worlds. If there was a children's party and I wanted to join in, I could take Amy, who was frequently on loan from Susan Blanchard. Amy was like a little doll and I loved to dress her in ribbons and bows. One time, I thought her hair was thinning and in such a mess, I had the whole lot cut off. She looked like a G.I., and Susan went mad. The thing about hair, of course, is that it grows and, the following year, it sprouted out thicker and lusher than ever before. Susan telephoned to thank me.

Sayonara was long and drawn out, although, when it was over, everyone had to say how marvellous it was. We had one more drink, said our farewells and then drifted off to search for the car. It was no easy task – they were parked bumper to elegant bumper in a long line that filled the drive. Finally we climbed in, Hank turned the ignition and, before he pulled away, he leaned over and kissed me very affectionately on the cheek.

'You're quite something, you know that,' he said.

'Well, of course I did,' I replied.

My launching had been quite a success and Hank talked happily all the way back on the winding roads that led to Malibu.

We were staying that summer at the Bel Air beach house that belonged to Linda Christian – a divorce gift from Tyrone Power – and it was there the following morning that I awoke to find a package waiting at my bedside. It was from Adrian and contained the four books of *The Alexandria Quartet*.

News of the terrible scene I made on the plane from Death Valley to Las Vegas quickly found its way back to Fonda – so quickly and so exaggerated, in fact, that once and for all, and in his own silent and secretive way, he decided to do something about my fear of flying.

He had read in a newspaper somewhere about a woman who had a phobia about elevators – which was awkward, because her office was on the twenty-seventh floor in a tower block and every day she had to walk the stairs. Then, after years and years of searching, she found a cure.

Fonda didn't tell me what it was, but one day, when he didn't have to go to the studio, he said he had a surprise for me – downtown in Los Angeles. We got in the car and off we set, the wide boulevards and well-watered greenery of Hollywood changing gradually into a landscape of small houses, like cubicles all packed tightly together. It was to one of those cubicles that I was taken, and there I was introduced to a hypnotist.

I gasped.

He was tall, young with striking features and egg-shell blue eyes. It was all very frightening. He looked like a pilot. He had that suave, easy manner, a reasssurance that is so sound and solid you immediately feel as if you are tottering at the brink of some awful disaster.

'How nice to meet you,' he said in a pleasant voice. 'Do come into my office.'

I gasped again.

'Come with me?' I asked Fonda.

Fonda glanced at the hypnotist.

'That'll be fine,' he said.

I reached out for Fonda's hand and, with mingled impatience and trepidation, we followed the man into the next room. He was already aware of my problem and so, as soon as we were seated, the treatment began.

'Look into my eyes,' he said. I did, and they were radiant. 'Look into my eyes ... you are going to sleep, you are entering a deep sleep ... you are dreaming ... you see clouds ... you are in the clouds ... you are in an airplane and you move freely through the clouds ... you are happy ...'

I was staring into his lovely blue eyes and wondering if the clouds were the same clouds the fortune teller had seen. My mind wandered on to something else, the hypnotist kept on talking and then, suddenly, I realized that the pressure from Fonda's hand had weakened. I turned to look at my husband. A broad smile had formed on his lips. His eyes were wide open and he was in a deep trance.

The hypnotist was horrified. I am one of those people who isn't susceptible to hypnosis, unlike Fonda, who was the perfect subject. He was drawn slowly back down to earth and was so relaxed and so thrilled by the experience, he instantly booked three more sessions. By the end of them, he had given up smoking and had learnt how to put himself to sleep in two seconds.

I never went again – and I never completely lost my fear of flying.

7 . Io, Io, Io

Strange though it may seem to some, I always feel most at home in a kitchen. At parties, I am drawn there as if to a magnet, to all the pots and pans in shiny rows, the herbs and spices in their little jars, or drying on strings over the stove. I breathe deeply and rejoice in the fusion of different smells. I adore the cookery books with their flour fingerprints, the refrigerator with its half-eaten chickens and bowls of fresh cream.

You can learn a great deal about people from their kitchen: if they are well organized, experimental, energetic or, as was clearly the case with Paula and Lee Strasberg, a mixture of all three. It was the same mixture that had made the Actors Studio, which they created, so successful.

I was at their house one night, back once again in New York, the sound of voices and music far away and muffled in the adjoining room. I had already peeked into all the jars and bottles and, as I left the kitchen, I was suddenly struck by the most fascinating sight. At the far end of the corridor there was a high, arched window, and standing before it were two motionless figures in silhouette. It was like a Japanese Zen painting. The scene depicted the human form in opposites. One was tall, slightly bent and bird-like, a man who could have been a philosopher or an Oxford don. The woman by comparison was short, with gracefully flowing contours and the most beautiful and perfectly rounded bottom I had ever seen.

They turned and, as they walked towards me, I recognized Marilyn Monroe, whom I did know, and Arthur Miller, whom I didn't.

We greeted each other and talked about the summer for a few minutes. Marilyn had been staying at a house near by and at that time, while she was preparing herself for the film *Some Like It Hot*, she had been timid and rather edgy. But that had all passed; with Miller she seemed happy, more contented and very much in love – so much in love, she forgot to introduce me to him.

We parted. The next time we met they were married, and Marilyn was playing at being the good wife, staying at home, cooking meals and doing all sorts of things that she had never done before. A couple of times, after Fonda had finished work at the theatre, we went to the Millers' for supper. The men would talk shop and politics and Marilyn and I would talk recipes, although neither of us really knew what we were talking about. Once I complimented her on the salad dressing and she said she had put honey in it.

'I got it out of a magazine. I get everything out of magazines,' she said.

Marilyn was too self-absorbed ever to focus on me, although, like a lot of people, she was intrigued to know how Fonda and I got together.

'What's it like to be married to him?' she then asked.

'Marvellous,' I replied. 'We're both so completely different we have unusual things in common.'

Marilyn wasn't sure what to say to that. She just stared back. Her eyes were eager and searching. She was so short-sighted that, when she did focus on you, it made you feel as if you were the only person who really mattered to her. It was part of her charm, a tiny part, for she was charming in almost every way. She was gentle and fragile, like a dove, but I also sensed a certain ruthlessness, a hard, tough side that would take her wherever she wanted to go even though she was not sure where that might be.

Like a lot of people at that time and in that same world, Marilyn Monroe was so overcome by the American dream that it trapped her and finally made her very life into a cliché. Our needs and ideas were poles apart but, across the distance, I saw someone who was reaching out from a private and unknown despair. One day on the beach in Malibu, she took my hand and held it as if she was a child in need of help and protection. She was being protected by the Strasbergs and everyone else, but her deeper, psychological needs were far too confused for anyone to understand. She was already a big star; now she needed to find herself.

Arthur Miller must have loved Marilyn, but as a match they were anything but ideal. He wrote great things, like *Death of a Salesman*, but as a person he had a dimension missing. To me he seemed a completely cold fish. Fonda was similar, but somehow you could always reach him. You could always provoke him into warming up. I can't imagine what would have reached Miller, unless it was sex, or unless he thought he was going to do a Pygmalion transformation on Marilyn, which appeared highly unlikely. Even when she was in the kitchen cooking hamburgers, she was pouty and glamorous. She wore white satin dresses that hugged her curves and black boots. Her hair was the most vivid shade of blonde, sometimes with the dark roots just slipping into view. She loved white. Everything in the apartment was white – the carpets, the furnishings, the curtains. There were rows of books on the shelves, prints and paintings on the walls and classical music frequently on the stereo.

Because of Miller, Marilyn was trying to be artistic, an intellectual, although I'm sure that before they even met she had started to become mentally unbalanced. She desperately wanted a child; each time she had one of her several miscarriages it made her more distant and depressed. When things started to go bad in her marriage, I think Arthur Miller was the sort of man who would be tough, rather than kind.

After she died, in his confusion he brought out a play called *After the Fall* that told the story of an academic imprisoned in his marriage to a sex symbol. It was his own story, his and Marilyn's. He hated her because he had loved her, and was so haunted by her memory that he was trying to burn it out of his system by showing Marilyn as dull, impotent and violent. It was awful because she couldn't hit back and more awful because, even if it was partly true, it was only one part of Marilyn and not the whole. The play opened at a small, circular theatre off Broadway. I saw it and was horrified.

Marilyn, when I looked back, had obviously been doomed and was obviously very special. She had something deep inside, a soul like a beam of white light, and, whatever way she was pushed by her own ambitions and by others who were ambitious for her, that light kept shining through. At her death in 1962 everyone was devastated, but no one was surprised. It was just as if a light had been turned out.

When I wasn't peeping into other people's kitchens, I was spending more time in my own, cooking – well, sometimes: more often arranging menus for some future celebration.

We were in the closing months of 1958. Amy was back with Susan after spending the summer with us, Peter I didn't think about; and Jane had finally given up all notions of becoming an artist in Paris and had begun studying the Method at Lee Strasberg's Actors Studio. At first, Fonda didn't approve. It was all too modern and way out, but, as he watched his daughter, he slowly changed his mind.

Jane was marvellous, really gifted, and once she had committed herself to a career as an actress she started to glow even more as a woman. I remember one party where Salvador Dali couldn't keep his eyes off her. It was embarrassing. Everyone was embarrassed except Gala, Dali's wife, and she was too self-centred to notice. Dali was immensely self-centred himself. He was a complete schizophrenic, a genius, and he only talked about himself and his work. It was the era when he wasn't using a paint brush, but was shooting paint on to canvas with a gun. It was his only topic of conversation.

I, too, in my own way, had also moved into a new period. The number of society hostesses had always been few, and now I suddenly found myself in their ranks. I was talked about; I was noticed; I was mentioned in newspaper articles. Sometimes it seemed as if I got more coverage than my husband, and though Fonda had believed fervently that no publicity was bad publicity, there were occasions when he wasn't quite so sure. Once, he was described as the *Barone*, and he really hit the roof.

'Afdera, I don't care what you do, but this has got to stop,' he said. 'It's driving me crazy.'

'Hank, it's driving me crazy as well,' I replied.

It was perfectly true. It wasn't any of my doing. It was mainly due to the gossip columnist and party giver Elsa Maxwell, who was rarely letting a day go by without putting my name in print: Afdera was wearing this and that; the Fondas were here; the Fondas were there; Afdera was at this place and that place. I was fed up with it, not for the same reasons as Hank but because it was always nice and boring and never bitchy or particularly interesting. Once Elsa had got the ball rolling, of course, the other society writers thought they were missing out on something and joined in.

Some people actually paid those writers to have their names included in the gossip columns and, though I wasn't one of them, I was mentioned so often it must have looked that way. What they didn't know, in fact what few people did know, was that Elsa Maxwell had been watching me for a long time, way back when Lorian was a débutante in Venice and I was still a teenager. 'Don't underrate the little sister,' Elsa had said. 'She may not be beautiful, but she's got something.'

I am not sure why she had taken a fancy to me, but she had – and, oddly enough, it was not in the way that Elsa took a fancy to some women. She was ugly, wicked and amusing. She had an extraordinary power, and she was a well-known lesbian. She looked a bit like a man, she talked like a man and she had seduced some of the most famous married ladies of her time.

It was Elsa who had organized that Onassis voyage and Elsa who had made sure that I was invited. She even allowed me to stay in bed in the mornings while most of the other guests were up and tramping over the Greek ruins. There were always more sights to see after lunch and, for as long as I can remember, I have hated to do too much before noon.

Ten years had gone by and up I pop again in New York, married to the popular and talented Henry Fonda and suddenly the darling of Elsa Maxwell's gossip column. Elsa liked me just because she liked me and, in that respect, I have truly had a charmed life. When it comes to the crunch, there have always been some good people for me to lean on, secret nests where I could hide and lick my wounds. These are the people I cherish most. They know who they are – not necessarily rich or important, but genuine friends who have chosen me for no other reason than that they wanted to. At every stage and through every change I have made, my guardian angels have been there – and, because of it, I have been able to get away with murder.

So, with Hank going from a film to a play and on to another film, and receiving lots of awards in the process, and with me now a little centre of social activity myself, the old brownstone townhouse in New York was constantly buzzing – dinners where everyone sat in the celebrated Venetian dining-room, parties that were carefully planned, and parties that just happened spontaneously, which were often the most memorable.

The formal affairs were very formal. I never asked anyone to dress up, but everyone did: the men in dinner jackets and black ties, the ladies in all that glittered. It didn't matter who you were or what you had to offer, as long as you were noticed. It was a bit like *Dallas*, only twenty years earlier. The women who were older wanted to appear younger and the women who were younger were eager to be more sophisticated. It was fascinating, more fascinating than most of the plays on Broadway. Most of the people in those days simply *were* something. The act of actually trying to be something special almost guaranteed that one would fail. I didn't try and everything seemed to work out fine. The names were shuffled out at random around the long dining table. The guests appeared in their finery and I left everyone to get on with it. Once the table had been set and the help had arrived from the agency, the night rested in the hands of fate – and Fidalma, naturally.

About two hours before the early birds made their entrance, I would vanish into a hot bath. The creams and scents would follow, and then I would be faced with the wardrobe, where I surveyed the clutter of chiffons and frills like a child before a list of flavours in an ice cream store. To offset this awesome task, I would dance around the room, usually without any clothes on at all to the rhythm of the African Qualars – it was my favourite music.

One of the nicest things about organizing a social gathering was putting the various people together. I liked bizarre combinations, characters with something new to offer. Sometimes I would find myself with two separate groups, each as different in taste as vodka and tomato juice, but by the time the evening was through, we usually had the best Bloody Marys in New York. People made friends and stayed friends. I would like to know how many love affairs started and how many deals were born in the quieter corners on East 74th.

Nine times out of ten, everything went marvellously – though when it didn't, the result was just as memorable.

There was one evening when all the guests were talking heatedly about the Hungarian Revolution. Voices were raised, tempers wore thin and then one man marched up to another and angrily poked him in the chest.

'It's all because of you,' he snarled. 'It's because of you and people like you.'

The accuser was a man named Matthias, who worked as a correspondent for *Paris Match*, and the accused was the artist Brian Stonehouse – who hadn't said a word and who remained silent. He just turned his back and walked away.

Brian is as English as warm beer, rain in August and Big Ben – but simply no one thought so at the time. It was rumoured that he was a former member of the German ss who had fled to America with a new identity and started a new life. He never denied the rumour, which seemed to confirm it. He has a rather unique accent and even the name

Stonehouse sounds suspicious if you want it to.

I'm not sure why, perhaps intuition again, but, deep down, I didn't believe the gossip. Besides, the very idea of having a villainous Nazi seated at my dining table was so wonderfully outrageous I decided to enjoy it. The only problem was, Fonda began to worry.

'You ought to be careful of this man, Afdera,' he said one day.

'Brian? But why?'

'You know what they're all saying.' He paused, and then added cautiously: 'Well, they're saying he's an ex-Nazi.'

'I don't care if he is,' I answered. 'I can afford to have a Nazi if I want one.'

I was to learn much later – and not from his own lips – that, far from being a former member of the s s, Brian had used his skill with languages in the British secret service. At the age of nineteen, he was parachuted into France. He worked with the Resistance, was eventually captured and spent a number of years in some of the most notorious concentration camps. He did go to America to make a fresh start, not with a new identity, but with the old one. He never discussed the war and he never saw any need to explain himself.

That was probably why I liked him.

When we first met, he was doing a series of sketches of society women that were used on the programme covers at the Metropolitan Opera. He asked me if I would mind having a drawing done, I agreed, and we made arrangements to meet at his studio.

I sat and he started. Everything was going well, but then he asked me if he could put some cream on my face, 'to bring out the highlights'.

I went berserk.

'No,' I said indignantly. 'You certainly may not.'

His mouth dropped open, the cream remained on the shelf, and he finished his work in complete silence. He never explained himself, and I saw no need to explain myself – until now.

It actually had nothing to do with Brian Stonehouse, but another artist, a man by the name of René Bouché, whom I first met during the summer we had taken a villa at Cap Ferrat. René was a society figure, often the 'extra' man at parties, and, when he appeared at the house in New York, like all painters when they want to paint someone, he admired my bone structure and told me what a perfect model I would make. Fonda was delighted. At the time, he wanted the whole world to paint me, so off I went to the studio. It was a charming place, right on the top floor of the building next to the Plaza Hotel, overlooking the skating rink in Central Park.

The painter had said that he liked me in green, so I had brought three different dresses with me, one of which he chose. I changed, sat in the bay window and, with the winter sun throwing out a gentle light for the background, the work began. He was half hidden behind a large wooden easel, but still I could see the movement of his brush. It flew over the canvas in a sort of desperate urgency, his eyes flashing back and forth. It was like a pantomime and would have been extremely entertaining, except for one thing: the faster he painted, the more he panted. He was breathing heavily as if – well, I wasn't too sure, but it was *heav-i-ly*...

I ignored it. I pretended it was all in my imagination and continued to smile sweetly until the session was over. I went back the following day, dressed in the same dress and resumed my position in the window. I didn't say a word. I screwed my face into the correct expression and, as the brush started up again, so did René Bouché, panting and groaning until in the end, I was sure he was going to have an orgasm – or worse.

Once more, I acted as if I was deaf, but really I was quite upset. That night, I told Fonda what had happened and he said I wasn't to return. He was very caring, very understanding – and also very keen to see what the artist had produced. The next day, he went to the studio. He fell in love with the painting and immediately bought it. It was incomplete, but it was probably better that way. It captured the mood, unfinished, as much in life is left unfinished. At least the story had a happy ending for all three of us. For Fonda, because he was thrilled with the painting; for René Bouché because he sold it; and for me, because it was another of life's experiences.

In America my life was like one of those mirrored balls that revolve above dance floors, the chips of glass picking out odd colours, feelings and faces, and then moving on again. Every day was different, as each new day should be; I couldn't wake up desperate or depressed, even if I wanted to. For that brief period I was possessed by a calm, optimistic fatalism; just to be in New York, was to be in a perpetual state of astonishment. I was living between the shuffled pages of *Who's Who*, though, with my natural perversity, it often seemed that the people I most wanted to meet were either enemies of Fonda or had died just before our paths could cross.

There were exceptions, however, almost every night; such as Richard Burton appearing at twelve with his wife Sybil and then keeping us all amused singing Welsh songs until sunrise. It made me so envious because I couldn't sing any Italian songs. Sybil was full of laughter, had white hair and a very young face – and Burton was so hypnotic, so charismatic. In the end, he fell in love with his own charisma. When he met Elizabeth Taylor, all his red Celtic blood came bubbling to the surface: he lost control and then went totally gaga. Liz Taylor is a woman with great desires and passions: she is very animal and when she talked, it was about the most normal, everyday things, like food. When Burton and Taylor found each other it must have been like finding their own second self; their love and their needs were so powerful it destroyed them both.

Another woman with strong passions is Sophia Loren. The first time we spoke, Carlo Ponti had taken Fonda to one side and was whispering and shrugging in that Italian way, and, as soon as we were alone, Sophia did much the same.

'Darling,' she said. 'Is there any spaghetti in the house?'

'I beg your pardon?'

'Spaghetti ... have you got any spaghetti?'

'I don't think so,' I replied. 'I'm not really a spaghetti person.'

She looked heartbroken. 'You're not?' she gasped. 'Oh, my God ... I can't live without spaghetti ... I owe my life to spaghetti ...'

There was a long pause and then I said lightly: 'It's not for nationalist reasons, is it?'

'No, no, no, no, no ... I love spaghetti.'

I could have been sitting there with a heroin addict. Sophia seemed so miserable, I didn't know what to do; but then I had an idea.

'Perhaps my maid has got some,' I said. 'We can ask her.'

'She's Italian?'

'Yes.'

Relief flooded her face. 'Ah, Afdera, thank God. She must have some. I can't go another minute without some spaghetti.'

We set off for the kitchen.

Carlo Ponti was still gesturing wildly and Fonda was nodding and not saying very much. Ponti at first appeared to be a nice, cosy little man with a round face and a tiny hat, but as soon as he spoke you knew that, for him, business came first. He was constantly trying to raise money for films that would launch Sophia Loren further into orbit, and he was very good at it.

Sophia and I found Fidalma, a packet of spaghetti was discovered in a drawer and a big saucepan of water was soon boiling on the stove.

I went to see the men.

'We're cooking spaghetti, do you want some?' I asked.

'Sure,' Fonda replied.

'Not me,' said Mr Ponti. 'I can't stand the stuff.'

A year or so later – after my divorce from Fonda – Sophia and I were together in Italy, and on that occasion she went on and on about children. It was funny because, at the time, she still didn't have any.

'What about you, can you have children, Afdera?' she asked.

'And how,' I replied.

'But you haven't got any and you live alone, it must be terrible.'

'No, I prefer it,' I said.

Sophia couldn't work me out at all, although I think she finally came to the conclusion that, since I wasn't like her, I couldn't possibly be Italian.

Food seems to have figured rather strongly in my various exchanges – with Marilyn, with Liz Taylor, Sophia Loren. It wasn't that I was so interested in the subject, but I didn't give away very much of myself, and food at least was a meeting point.

For a long time, Gloria Vanderbilt – she was then married to Sidney Lumet – considered me merely frivolous and empty-headed. But one night, we both got sloshed and began to pour out all our hidden fears and feelings. When Fonda appeared, Gloria said: 'Hank, I thought you had married a silly, charming, amusing woman – but you know something, she has an inside, she has a soul.' It was a compliment indeed, especially from a woman like Gloria. She can paint, write, design – she can do anything.

Occasionally I would open up and talk, but really I much preferred to listen – to Peter Ustinov, a man worth listening to in about twenty different languages; or to David Niven, who was a gentleman, but with a nice and naughty twinkle; even to Annibale Scotti, who made a habit of turning up when he was least expected.

Numerous strangers would also find their way to our doorstep – sometimes just because New York is that sort of city and sometimes as a result of an absurd game that Fonda and I played to keep ourselves amused. At most places, we knew everyone and everyone knew us, but, when we did go somewhere obscure, once in a while we would pretend that we weren't together and then see who could acquire the most admirers. It was terribly unfair. By the time Fonda had extracted one telephone number, my number had been scribbled hastily into several little black books. For each new friend I had a new story and then, in the days that followed, there was chaos, over the telephone wires and, with the more adventurous, right there in our own hallway. On one memorable occasion, Fonda answered the door to a rather well-known English politician. He recognized Fonda, Fonda recognized him, and that was that.

It was wicked and harmless, and at those things Fonda never got angry. As far as *other* men were concerned, there was only one time when I saw him get violent – and that was with a total stranger. It took place outside an hotel. I was going through a revolving door and a man got me trapped on purpose and made me go round again. Fonda's expression didn't change. He walked straight up to the man, pulled back his long right arm and punched him on the jaw. I was horrified, speechless. The man staggered away rubbing his chin and then Fonda began to feel sorry for himself.

'That was all your fault,' he complained. 'You were making eyes at him.'

'I certainly wasn't.'

'I've never hit anyone in my life,' he moaned.

'Except me.'

'That's different,' he said. 'We're married.'

I looked at Hank and Hank looked at me. The same thought was going through our minds. Nothing was said, nothing ever was said, but we both knew that we had reached a turning-point – the last turning-point.

8 . *Life and Death*

There was nothing feminine about Henry Fonda. He had no special intuition or anything like that. He never tried to be a wizard and predict what was going to happen – with one remarkable exception. It was before we were married, during my first trip to New York. We were having lunch at a very nice restaurant and sitting at a large table in the very centre of the room was a group of lively, talkative men, most of them with their jackets over the backs of their chairs.

'You see that man there?' Fonda said. He pointed out a young man with a pleasant smile and lots of hair. I nodded and Fonda became all wise and knowing as he added: 'One day he's going to be the President.'

I glanced over for a second look.

'Impossible,' I said. 'He's a baby. He's fourteen years old.'

Fonda just smiled.

'How do you know?' I then asked.

'I've been wrong so many times, I just know that this time I'm right,' he replied.

Fonda was so serious I knew he wasn't pulling my leg. I took a third little peep. The very idea was absurd. Politicians have to be old and asthmatic and the man in the restaurant was too young and really much too good-looking.

Before I knew it, it was 1960. John Kennedy was the Democratic candidate for President; I remembered that it was Fonda who had seen it coming. In the past my husband had gone out electioneering for Adlai Stevenson, who was never elected, and now he put his energies into the Kennedy campaign.

So did I. Like the wives in California who were always raising money for various charities, I began to help organize things – parties, balls, galas, anything that would bring in money for the campaign fund. It was enthralling, it was usually successful and I loved every minute of it. John and Jackie were the golden couple and everyone wanted to help. John was so obviously a winner and Jackie had a special style and the right image for the new decade. When they were in New York, they stayed at the Carlyle, close to East 74th, and often appeared at the house for a late supper. Hank advised Jack not to strain his voice. 'It's cost people the election before now,' he said. He told Bobby Kennedy, the campaign manager, to make sure they had the best sound equipment. 'Whatever you do, don't shout.' The Kennedys listened like nice college boys and were grateful for all Hank's suggestions. They liked him a lot, and so did Jackie.

Jack was enchanting. He had an enormous amount of curiosity and liked nothing more than meeting new people with fresh ideas. For me, politics was then unimportant, but with Jack Kennedy it was more of a challenge. Throughout that period he was taking cortisone for an old injury; in those days the drug was less refined and gave the taker an extraordinary amount of adrenalin – in every department. The very first time we met, he shook my hand and immediately started to ask me questions about the Italian President. Now at that particular moment I didn't know who it was – they change every five minutes in Italy – but somehow I managed to turn the question around and he told me. I then said something about Yugoslavia, and what I said was dead right and appeared very clever, though, naturally, it was a complete fluke. I actually knew nothing about Yugoslavia except that before the war my mother and father used to go there to visit friends who had a divine house that had since been confiscated by Tito. I didn't know why but it had seemed unreasonable.

Jack was so interested that on future occasions, I began to make things up. I'm sure he believed me, and because he believed me they became true. That was my big mistake. I had set myself up as an observer of European affairs and had to start reading the newspapers and watching the news so that I wasn't caught out. I began getting up earlier and it was such hard work. I can't imagine how I did it. I would meet Jack Kennedy at a party or a reception and instead of being amusing, I had to be serious. '*Yeow*', he'd say, '*yeow*'. He had a very special way of talking and in the end, of course, everyone was talking the same way. I suppose I would have joined in, but my own peculiar accent was as permanent as a tattoo: an English that was vaguely Italian, Italian that was slightly German, a German with shades of the Irish. It had all been

acquired from a series of different nannies; it wasn't my fault. Mama
and Baroness Stockhausen spoke French, Lorian and Simba spoke English and the servants spoke Venetian. Perhaps Sophia Loren was right:
I wasn't Italian at all.

It was the day after that first conversation with Jack Kennedy that I
found myself face to face with Jackie (dear Jack Peacock would have
been in ecstasy). She was the embodiment of *Jaws*. 200,000 teeth and
two cunning eyes, one on either side of her head.

'I hear you met Jack,' she said. 'He thought you were charming.'

'Really?'

'Really.'

She also had an incredible way of talking: very civilized but with a
mass of undercurrents. We discovered that we had mutual friends in
Italy, though all I could focus on was her amazing mouth with its rows
of sharp little teeth. Our eyes never met. Mine are rather close together
and, with Jackie's being so far apart, the only way we could have looked
at each other would have been if I had danced about from side to side –
and I wasn't going to do that. There was no chemistry between us. The
reason for that, quite simply, was that Jackie had got it into her head
that I was secretly seeing her husband and that I had known him longer
than I really had. Even if that had been true, it could still only have
been a rumour as far as Jackie was concerned and one would have
expected the future First Lady not to bother herself with gossip.

The months peeled away until January 1961. It was time for the
famous inauguration. Hank and I were invited to all events, although
Hank couldn't go because he was in a play. I went to Washington with
a group of friends who had been invited from New York. We stayed in
a marvellous hotel and from the moment we arrived we never stopped
moving. On the first day the famous swearing-in ceremony was to be
held.

I got up that morning after a late party the night before and looked
out of the window. It was the coldest winter in America for thirty years.
The wind was blowing across the wide open spaces, the trees were heavy
with snow. It looked like orange blossoms. I glanced back at my cosy
bed and the large television that stood at the foot of it and there was
not a moment of doubt in my mind as to what I was going to do. I
didn't feel the slightest guilt. I ordered the most enormous breakfast,
climbed under the covers, tucked myself in and watched history being

made from the comfort of my warm bed, while all my friends stood freezing in the cold a mile away. Everyone was wearing a hat except Jack Kennedy. He didn't even have a coat, and seemed so young and vulnerable.

There now followed three days of celebrations. Everything was organized, with buses reserved to take us to all the different parties and balls. The night I remember best was the last night, when Jack was to give another speech at the Armoury, a vast hall with tiers of seats disappearing into the heavens and a large, open area the size of Wembley Stadium. Jack and Jackie were miles away in a special box. She was all in white and absolutely impeccable. Everyone was dressed up to the nines and most uncomfortable on the hard wooden benches. There were ambassadors and their wives and near by in the crowd I could see several people I knew: Marietta Tree, the former companion of Adlai Stevenson, Evangeline Bruce, who would eventually come to London when her husband David became the American ambassador to Britain; and Pamela Churchill, the former wife of Randolph Churchill, who would later marry Averell Harriman, a diplomatic envoy for several American administrations. I was with a small group from New York, with Fifi Phell as our mother hen.

Suddenly I felt very claustrophobic, so I left everyone and wandered off alone down the steep wooden steps. My shoes, as always, were too tight and so I took them off and carried one in each hand. People were moving in every direction, as thick as ants, and so many that it was impossible to focus on anyone. Suddenly, I turned around and there, amongst all the noise and the chatter and the pushing, I saw a small, sunny figure who, at that moment, looked just as lost as I was. It was the new President, and he appeared to be completely on his own.

'My God,' I said.

'Hi,' Jack replied – very American.

'What are you doing here?'

'I had to get away,' he said.

'So did I. My shoes are hurting, there're too many people and I can't wait to go back to Joe Alsop's to have some spaghetti.'

As I finished speaking, the crowd closed in. Everyone recognized the new President and, as they did so, I backed away and returned to my seat, and there I remained until the end of the ceremony.

When we managed to get out of the Armoury, a limousine that had been put at our disposal took a few of us to the journalist Joe Alsop's magical house in Georgetown. All the houses in the old part of Washington are very English, except Joe's, which was more *avant-garde* and far more interesting. Joe had built a Japanese garden in the hall with miniature bonsai trees and stepping stones that climbed down to a glass-walled living room. It was marvellous to be able to relax and at the same time relive the strange meeting with Jack that came flooding back into my mind. It was such an odd, unique thing to have happened. He was now perhaps the most powerful man in the world, yet there he was, so normal, so natural that one reacted by being natural oneself. I had the feeling that he was so alone, really alone. That tiny moment of meeting out of the blue was such a special thing to have happened, I kept it to myself.

'Come on, Afdera, you're the Italian,' Joe called a short while later. 'You must be the expert on spaghetti.'

'Oh, my God, I'm hopeless,' I replied, 'but let's give it a try.'

Barefoot in my long dress, I walked into the kitchen and put a large saucepan on to boil. When the spaghetti was just about cooked the doorbell rang.

'Oh, Christ, who can this bore be coming at this time of night?' Joe asked annoyed.

He climbed up to the entrance hall and I followed and peeked from behind his back while he opened the door. There was a small figure standing there in the dark with bowed shoulders and a big grin. Joe was so stunned he couldn't speak.

'I hear there's some spaghetti here,' Jack Kennedy said.

Joe responded: 'Mr President . . . ?'

'You mean now I'm the President I can't have any spaghetti?'

Joe now opened his arms and greeted his old friend and brought him in. It was delightful. The spaghetti was disgusting, but we all huddled together in the drawing-room. Jack took his jacket off, sat on the sofa and we all sat around him on the floor. His adrenalin was so high, he didn't stop talking, though he remained articulate and relaxed. One of the few things that stuck in my mind was his comment on Eisenhower, his presidential predecessor. The campaign against Nixon had been a tough one, but when Jack finally won and it came to the ceremony where the outgoing President passes over the keys to the White House, Jack found a kindness and humanity in Eisenhower that he had not before seen.

The night vanished. The dawn came up and the glow from the sun bathed the room in a warm golden light. It was time for us to go home. Jack left with his Secret Service man and suddenly it occurred to me: Where could Jackie be?

The next time I saw the First Lady was at a Schlumberger display at Tiffany's, where I had gone with Brian Stonehouse. Jackie was mingling with the guests, shaking hands here and there and having a few words with each person. Suddenly, we were facing each other. She shook my hand, her 200,000 teeth disappeared, and she moved on.

'What's happened?' Brian asked.

'I don't know, she's just a *macaca*.'

'A what?'

'A *macaca* is just a *macaca*,' I replied. 'Why don't you ask Gore Vidal? He would know. He loves Venice, and some of our favourite slang. I'm sure he would agree with me.'

During the Kennedy period, I went through a great number of changes. As a social animal, I had reached the top of the mountain, and from there I could see it all for what it was: just another experience and one that I observed without allowing it to get under my skin. I often appeared frivolous, because deep down I was dissatisfied with my life, and subconsciously I yearned to stretch my wings and fly over new ground. I played a role and appeared comfortable as a society lady, but I was just as happy to be alone. It didn't matter how exotic the function or important the guests, the best moment of my day was usually when I closed the bedroom door and fell headlong across the bed. I liked other people's kitchens, but I loved my own bed. It was my island, my sanctuary, the hideaway where I could think in peace – thoughts that were suddenly dense and complex and in contrast with all the exciting stuff going on outside the window.

I had started to look in, rather than always looking out, and what I saw both frightened me and made me steel myself for a tremendous challenge. My mother was dying and, when she did, I knew I was going to feel lost and empty; yet, instead of that making me want to stay on the easy path and cling tighter to my husband, it made me want to strike out on my own. Fonda and I had been married for nearly four years, but in many ways we were still strangers. I had found myself playing the role of the spoilt wife, the superficial butterfly, and, like an actress on the stage, I just kept playing it. Fonda was a serious, sensitive, fair and balanced man, but, sadly or ironically, I responded to those qualities by drawing on the negative aspects of my personality. We didn't drift apart; but we had different friends, different interests, we were from different generations and the gap was starting to show. It could have been the recipe for a perfect marriage, but it wasn't. Hank was an idealist in search of a Shangri-la shared by two and I wasn't ready to make such a massive commitment. I was too young, I was discovering myself, I was too deeply affected by all the many changes that were suddenly taking place. I was in tune with the present. The 1960s were with us like a hungry lion and everything I was feeling instinctively my husband was too old and too well established to appreciate fully.

The thoughts passed in and out of my head and kept me in a constant state of mental turmoil. The presidential election campaign had filled the calendar, the days were hectic and, perhaps typically, I added to the confusion by bringing my mother to New York to have a series of tests at the Memorial Hospital. It was the best in the world for the treatment of cancer and, although she did have the tests and she did have the treatment, Mama had her own private reasons for making the trip.

She arrived in the worst snowstorm of the winter. The weather was bitter, the roads were icy and it took hours to reach the airport. Luckily, I had become good friends with the manager of Alitalia and he arranged for Mama to go through the landing formalities on the aircraft and, when she stepped off, it was straight into the car. On the journey back, Fonda took her hand and, as they sat there, there was a nice, silent rapport between them.

Mama was so independent, she insisted on staying at an hotel. We booked a suite at the Plaza, which was close to the hospital; she went for treatment each day and then a car would bring her to the house, usually to lock herself away with my husband. They talked for hours. The general theme seemed to be my complicated nature, although the longer Mama stayed the more she and Fonda enjoyed each other's company simply for its own sake. When Mama was lucid, she was bright, intelligent, witty and a marvellous companion. Then, something would switch off in her mind and she would spend days staring at a fly as it moved over the walls of her room.

In New York Mama remained normal and it wasn't very long before she reached the conclusion that Henry Fonda was the perfect gentleman, even if he wasn't a Catholic. With that established, she sat herself down one afternoon and I could see by the look in her eyes that she wanted to have one of her serious talks. We were in her hotel room, on her own ground.

'Afdera, you know he's a very good man, your husband,' she said. 'You're very fortunate.'

I nodded.

'He is the sort of man you will always be able to rely on,' she continued. 'He is strong, he has a good character. I only wish that I had got to know him before.'

I still didn't speak. I didn't know what to say. Mama's voice softened and she suddenly seemed sad. 'I was very wrong to be against your marriage, I can see that now,' she sighed. 'I should have been with you. It should have been done properly.'

She suddenly seemed so tiny and old, and her sadness made me want to weep – for her, for me, for the world. What she wanted was so little and what she said about Fonda so true. I could feel it in the depths of my being but, even as I agreed with what she said, and all she was about to say, I still knew that for Fonda and me time was running out.

There was a long, quiet moment and then Mama said: 'Afdera, will you do this for me – will you marry this man in the Church?'

'Yes,' I answered automatically. 'Yes, of course I will.'

'It will make me so happy. It's the only thing I want,' she paused again, ' – that and your happiness.'

Tears had sprung into her eyes. We reached out and held each other, and, as usual, I felt completely confused. Mama had a special affection for me which she didn't have for her other three children. I didn't know why and I had never been able to return that affection with the passion it deserved. We were such opposites, physically, psychologically, emotionally; she had cut herself off from life and lived like a nun, while I, as if in reaction to this, had always followed worldly pursuits – travel, culture, society, men. I had always been haunted by the ghost of my father; in a different, more intense way, I was haunted by the ghost of Mama. She was there, but not there, like a vision across a deep, echo-filled chasm, something too distant for me to ever reach. Lorian, probably because she was a mother herself, did feel a closeness with Mama and could never understand why I didn't. It was this lack of understanding that contributed much to the division between us.

Mama continued to sob, only now it was with happiness. I gave her my word that I would marry Fonda in church and I have never stopped feeling guilty because I didn't. Her request was the real reason why she had come to America; with the mission complete, she abandoned the hospital treatment and arranged to return to Italy. I took her to the airport. She climbed on board the aeroplane in her quiet, dignified way and, when the plane took off, the tears began to roll down my cheeks. I knew I would never see Mama again. She stayed with Lorian and it was with her, soon after, that she died.

When the news came, all I wanted was to be on my own. Grief for me is something private. I lock it away in a little box and I only think back over the joyous things in my memory. I open the box much later, frequently when I should be rejoicing, and then all my sorrow comes pouring out. As I said, I always cry at weddings, never at funerals.

When my mother died, Fonda had stage commitments, so it was alone that I went to join my family in Rome. From there, we travelled with Mama to San Trovaso, where she was to be entombed in one of the large stone walls on the estate. It is the tradition to leave the casket open, but Mama had become so ravaged it was sealed before being put in the drawing-room for the servants and village people to come and pay their last respects. Mama slipped away quietly, no fuss, no ceremony. It was as if she was in a hurry to pass into the next life.

That night, candles were left burning like sentinels over the coffin, the eerie glow throwing shadows across the dark paintings that shrouded the walls. Nothing had changed since my childhood. Alone in my old bedroom, with all that was familiar around me, I could hear the house echoing as if Mama and all our ancestors called out from the past.

We had long memories, the Franchettis, but the way ahead was unknown, virgin soil like the lands once explored by our father. Unlike him, however, we were completely unprepared for what the future had in store. Lorian already had financial problems, Nanuck soon would have, and one day so would I. The wealth that had always been an ocean had vanished into a trickling stream, and the stream was running dry. In some ways Mama was fortunate not to see the decline. She wasn't from a different generation but from a different century. The world had moved on and, like many old families, we were suddenly dinosaurs stranded in the wrong age.

I was brought up with a house full of nannies and servants. For a long time I thought that was the way everyone lived. As a teenager I ran away to become an actress, and a maid and a chauffeur went with me. I usually got my entrances wrong, I forgot my lines – and everyone forgave me. I was used to getting away with things. My education through the war had been haphazard at best. I was allowed to run wild and I never acquired the habit of concentration and concerted effort. I have always been able to handle sickness and suffering more easily than boredom, and that stems from my childhood. Life was easy, too easy. I knew the social rules, but I didn't know how to take care of myself. Unfortunately, making a career was not part of my upbringing and the thought of taking a job was foreign to me – I didn't know how to go about it. I was twenty-seven when my mother died and I was still fast asleep. Waking was to be a painful process.

Such thoughts, like the changes in my fortunes, came later, but as I lay sleeplessly in my bed in San Trovaso, what I was suddenly thinking about was a few trivial little objects that were important to me – a glass bird, a china dish, a silver box, things of no great value but which I wanted to keep. Mama was lying dead in her coffin, the house was cold with grief, yet I knew there were going to be petty squabbles over who owned what. Mama said this ... Mama said that ... I could see it coming and, with that in mind, I slipped out of bed and made my way quietly to the drawing-room.

My nightdress was white and so was Lorian's. We studied each other through the candlelight, we passed like two phantoms and neither of us said a word.

I returned to my room, closed the door and stared out at the moon and stars framed by the window. I had taken the glass bird and now had an impulse to throw it against the wall. I could be reckless, thoughtless, frivolous and sometimes superficial, but never grasping, greedy, small-minded, mean. I was much better than that. And much worse. I held the little bird in the palm of my hand and gazed at it in the moonlight. I decided not to break it. I kept it as a token of the shame that now gripped me, a shame that would never quite go away. I climbed into bed and, although I didn't sleep very well, I wasn't at all tired when I awoke. If anything I felt numb. My sorrow was locked safely away and, when I glanced at myself in the mirror, the person I saw had the blankness of a statue. I was empty, a freshly glazed jar waiting to be filled with new emotions, new experiences, a new love. I dressed in clothes that I would wear that one day and never again.

There was a chill in the air when we gathered for the burial. It was a quiet affair, just family, a few villagers, the servants. Baroness Stockhausen was very pale and had tears in her eyes. So did Ernesto, the gardener. Mama had loved her trees and flowers and it was with him that she planned the estate. Lorian, in black instead of ghostly white, looked detached, while Nanuck seemed older.

Like Ernesto, all the servants were ancient and had been with Mama for so long they had a fondness for her that they would never feel for anyone else. It was the end of an era in so many ways. The little scene with Mama being interred like a pharaoh in a stone wall seemed like both a memorial to one age and the beginning of another. The world was changing and I was changing with it. I had started to see others, not only myself.

During the night before the funeral a bell slowly chimed in the village and that more than anything brought back all my memories of childhood. Bells were always ringing in San Trovaso, but it was the slow bell that told you someone had died. It was a community of old people and so I heard it often. It was a part of life and, from a very young age, I was aware of death.

The first dead person I actually saw was a nun at the Sacred Heart Convent. She was lying in state and all the girls had to file past. Candles were burning, the light was shadowy and mysterious, and when I reached the casket I peered in and was horrified. The woman was shrunken and yellow, she looked more devilish than divine. I was so shocked I screamed and was immediately chastised.

The encounter with the dead nun made a great impression on me and the experience, perhaps more than any other, helped shape my personality. When I said my prayers that night, I asked for all the usual blessings and then added an extra message: I had decided that I never wanted to grow old, ever. Naturally, while I expected God to help in this matter, I knew he had a lot of other problems to think about and, if I was going to achieve my goal, I would also have to work at it myself.

I did exactly that. From that day on, instead of being serious and conscientious, I was breezy and carefree. In time it became a habit, and then it became me. I wasn't particularly disobedient and wilful, contrary to Lorian's regular reports to Mama, but I was lazy and rather nonchalant. I was one of those children whose teachers always said that they 'could do better'. But I never did, and I rarely lasted very long at each new school. I was 'delicate' and had to be brought home to continue my studies with a variety of governesses, Austrian, Irish, English, and all with their own unique methods of education and discipline.

They came, those ladies, to pass on all the knowledge of the universe, and the first thing I always learned was how to skip classes.

The reason I was considered delicate was because as a small child I had contracted polio. There was an epidemic, the gardener's daughter died and my childhood friend Andriana Marcello underwent many operations over the years. After one spell in hospital in New York, she stayed with Fonda and me to convalesce. She was then married to an American, the artist Timothy Hennessy; like my own marriage, it didn't last. Andriana and I have always been close; our destinies have been remarkably parallel.

My cure from polio was the result of Mama's belief in natural medicine. I was given the 'Sister Kenny' remedy, which was homoeopathic. I was constantly sipping strange herbal drinks and every day for a whole year a woman came from Treviso to massage my legs. When I started to get better, it was Ernesto who made me a special machine for exercise. It was marvellous. It was a little green box shaped like a boat with a mast and flags, pedals and three wheels. It was so well made, it was still there when Mama died. As the only son, Nanuck inherited the house and, when he moved in with his children, they tried it and were terribly disappointed. They had shiny racing bikes and the wooden three-wheeler was pedestrian by comparison.

In some ways, my illness had been good for Mama. She was so concerned, she forgot herself and put all her energies into my recovery. Papa had died a short time before and her grief was so great that her first reaction had been to abandon us all. We went to stay with the Duke Amedeo d'Aosta, another giant like Papa, and his best friend, while Mama went to Ethiopia, where she remained at the expense of the Italian Government for an entire year. I'm not sure why.

My father was highly respected among the tribesmen in the north of the country and was considered the one man with enough influence to unite those people in any confrontation with the British. It was for that reason that Papa was held in high esteem by Mussolini and why his death would be expedient for his enemies.

It was Mama's second journey to Africa. The first had been when Papa was assumed missing and she arranged a small expedition to set out and find him. She did find him, sleeping under canvas with an Abyssinian princess. Mama entered the tent and screamed at the princess, and the girl responded by cursing Mama, her children, and her children's children. Legend has it that at this point the princess stood up, stark naked, left the tent and vanished into the sunrise.

Mama forgave Papa – she always did – and together they returned to Italy. Their romance was really quite extraordinary. Not only was he old enough to be her father, he was *very* close to Mama's mother, Moceniga Mocenigo, in her time a celebrated wit whose court of admirers included Kaiser Franz Josef and the poet D'Annunzio, a man who was as bald as an egg and who, when I was a child visiting Grandma, would give me chocolates in boxes made of solid silver. He was a war hero, a womanizer and completely fascinating.

'Why don't you have any hair?' I once asked.

'Why? Because I play billiards,' he replied.

Papa wasn't the boy next door but the young man who lived across the Grand Canal. Between his adventures in Africa and at the North Pole he had watched Mama grow up and, when he decided that he wanted to marry her, he took her for a walk along the little dock at the Palazzo Rocca and proposed. Mama instantly said no and Papa, who didn't know the meaning of the word, picked her up, stepped into the canal and plunged her head beneath the water. After the third ducking she breathlessly agreed to be his bride.

Socially it was a step down the ladder. Mama, a Rocca, was a countess and Papa was a mere baron from a family raised to the aristocracy only a century before and through an ancestor who was said – perhaps ironically – to keep the best pigs in Italy. The irony was that the barony, the humblest of titles, was generally conferred on people with Jewish antecedents – a dubious honour. Having money, of course, was essential and the Franchettis had been amassing riches for a thousand years.

That was my father's family history, and I'm sure my mother never gave it a moment's thought. She grew to love her strange husband and, when he died, a melancholia so overwhelmed her that she was carried away into a quiet and gentle madness. She returned from Ethiopia as if she had never been away, and collected her children. Once more she picked up the reins of the household, something she did with considerable detachment but with an eye for form and tradition. She imposed the same laws of etiquette that she had grown up with and we passed through each day as if the hands on the clock had stood still. The way I spoke and the way I held myself were as important as, if not more so than, my being well lettered. This harmonized with my natural propensity for idleness and, though I was an enthusiastic reader, the result was that I would go through life having to fill the gaps in my knowledge with a mixture of charm and fantasy.

One of the few rules was that we all sat down to have lunch together at precisely 1.00 pm each day. It was like eating in a restaurant – the table formally set, two maids serving and a menu with a set dish for each day of the week. My favourite dish contained anchovies cooked in a magic sauce that was invented by our chef. The smell has often returned to me with its memories of the past, but the taste was so unique I have never found it again anywhere in the world.

After lunch, Mama, my sisters, Baroness Stockhausen and the governess – for a long time an Irish lady by the name of Miss Rooney – would retire to the drawing-room to take coffee. I would disappear and, inevitably, Lorian would be sent to find me.

'Mama's upset. This is the only time we have together and she wants you back in the drawing-room. Now.'

'I'm coming.'

'Now.'

'I'm coming. But do I have to? I want to read.'

'Come down immediately.'

I was about five years old before I spoke my first word and for the next ten years Lorian stated continually that she had preferred me when I was unable to say anything. That doesn't really do her justice, for she was an acute observer and had the knack of making magnificent quips on the spur of the moment. For example, when I was about sixteen there came an evening when I was dancing with a boy at an open-air dance in Venice. It was in a square paved in small square tiles. Lorian was my chaperone. The event passed without incident and, when we arrived home, Mama asked me if I had enjoyed myself. My sister answered for me:

'She certainly did, Mama, she never left the square she was dancing on.'

On the days when I managed to avoid afternoon coffee I would often run off to play with the mangy pack of dogs that roamed the estate. There were many, and all had names that began with the letter T: Timmy, Tommy, Tiny, Tousa, Toffee, Tart, nearly all English for some reason. There was also a Siamese cat called Maua, with brilliant green eyes. She was very independent and most unaffectionate: a real Franchetti. She slept in a basket coiled up like a snake and went with us whenever we went to stay at another house or with other members of the family, which was so often it seemed as if life was a permanent preparation for the next holiday.

When I wasn't playing with the animals, I was in the library, reading not only the books that were forbidden but everything there was. The collection was widely diverse and, if I gained any learning at all, it was there in the library. For a long time I read two books simultaneously, going from one to the other and then starting again when I finished. One was *Gone With the Wind* by Margaret Mitchell. The other was *The Well of Loneliness*, Radclyffe Hall's complex story about a woman who gradually realizes she is a lesbian. I liked it best. It was beautifully written, it made me think about life and it described feelings and emotions I didn't know existed. In our family everything to do with sex was strictly taboo and when I did finally ask Mama if it was possible for one woman to fall in love with another she said it wasn't possible and if it happened, it was only an illness.

Of course no one told me anything about the curse and when I grew older and suddenly found myself with my first period I thought I was dying. I ran screaming into Lorian's room.

'What shall I do? What shall I do?'

'Take a laxative.'

In the country in those days taking a laxative was the panacea for everything from a broken arm to a brain haemorrhage.

I had no doubt been misbehaving the day before and Lorian was punishing me by treating my distress with amusement. Something told me it was one of those problems I couldn't take to Mama and so I had to wait until Simba got home. By then I was in a dreadful state of nerves, but Simba's serenity and soft voice were calming and I sat there quietly as she went through a beginner's guide to the facts of life. It was all rather abstract. Simba didn't know a great deal about such things, even if she was a nurse, and, once I knew I wasn't going to die, I lost interest.

It was a part of growing up and that was something to avoid.

In some ways, Lorian and I were similar. I was always both afraid of and respectful towards her. Simba was easier to love, but far more difficult to know. There was an air of mystery and isolation about her, as if she looked out upon a landscape that no one else could see. She spent all her money on trees to forest the estate and, although she never had boyfriends, she did have a confessor, an elderly priest, whom she saw at least once a week. I was intrigued to know what she confessed, for she never did anything wrong. She just went through life with equanimity, helping others and asking nothing for herself. People often liked Lorian and me because we were more lively: Lorian was a beauty and I was a curiosity. But those who preferred Simba – Grandmama Moceniga Mocenigo was one – had feelings for her that ran far deeper. Her death was a tragedy for us all; though perhaps a greater tragedy was to be found in the fate of the small mark she had tried to leave behind her: the eight hundred trees she had planted became diseased and had to be cut down.

That first encounter with the facts of life came after the war, and by then we had all lived through those terrible years – terrible on reflection, for at the time I was far more fascinated than frightened. To me, the air raids were like a fireworks display and I would spend hours at the window watching the tracers dance across the sky. Since our house was rather large and had such a unique shape, the pilots used it as a marker. It was over us that they dropped the harmless flares that lit the way to their target ahead. When I saw the flares and heard the whine of falling bombs, I knew we weren't going to be hit.

Only once do I remember the silence, a massive silence as if the whole countryside was holding its breath; then there was the loudest explosion I have ever heard. Every pane of glass in the house was shattered, and when I ran outside I could see the fires spreading across the town seven miles away. It was Holy Friday 1944. It was a daylight raid, and the bombers had mistaken Treviso for the industrial centre at Tarvesium. Several thousand people were killed, all Italian civilians – only two Germans. A small school was hit and all the children died. The hospital was all but demolished. Simba was by then the head nurse, Lorian was a student nurse; both were on duty and, miraculously, both survived. Most of their friends perished. Simba had always been quiet, but now

LEFT Jane Fonda and me on Torcello
Fonda's photograph of me at Leptis Magna and
(*below right*) together in Tripoli, Libya

(*Above*) The painting that helped bring Fonda and me together and (*below*) two paintings by Fonda which I still treasure: the one on the left was painted when he was angry

Venice well before noon – taken by my friend Ugo Mulas

Showing a model what shot we wanted, San
Giorgio, Venice, also taken by Ugo Mulas

With the Italian film director Luchino Visconti

TOP With Gianni Agnelli and Sonny
Marlborough, and (*below*) with Harry

At the Summer Palace in Peking; (*above*) with
John Bailey on Bali and (*below*) me by John

With Peter Thorneycroft, President Pertini of Italy and Charles Forte; and (*below*) with 'the Hambleden boys' at their brother's wedding – Lorenzo, Bernardo, Nicholas and Alexander

The Bridge of Sighs, Venice, photographed by Clifford Thurlow

she became completely withdrawn. Outwardly she seemed tranquil but inside her nerves never recovered. She developed anorexia and never ate properly again until the day she died.

Her death came a little more than ten years later. I was a young woman off enjoying the world. When I returned to Rome and first saw Simba, I couldn't believe it was my sister. She had become so tiny and so thin that her body below the bedsheet looked no bigger than that of a small cat. She was weak from her loss of appetite and wasting away with tuberculosis. Neither Lorian nor I was afraid of catching the infection and we spent many hours and many days in the isolation ward at the Santa Margherita Hospital. Often we just sat in silence, as if our presence and our strength would somehow combine and put the life force back into our sister. Deep down we both knew that it was Simba's love and goodness that held the family together and that, without her, the future would be a darker, more barren place.

I gave Simba my blood, I fed her soup as if she was a child and we ate from the same spoon. I didn't catch the disease, but Lorian did; and Lorian was pregnant with her third child. She too had to go into isolation. She was told by the doctors to terminate the pregnancy: if she didn't, she or the baby was likely to die during the birth. Lorian never even considered the suggestion. She had her baby, she didn't die, and Luca was a bright, healthy little boy who would grow up to look like Simba.

By then, Simba was at rest in a stone drawer in the stone wall at San Trovaso. She had remained calm and peaceful throughout those last long days, though in her final hours she was gripped by a sudden panic. She cried out: 'I don't want to die. I haven't been a bad person . . . please God, let me live.' It was the unhappiest moment of my life. It was even worse for Lorian. Simba and Lorian were born ten months apart and were like *rouge* and *noir*, but had a very deep and special relationship.

Apart from that one horrific day when Treviso was bombed, the major effect the war had on our lives was that the house was requisitioned by the Germans. At first, Mama was beside herself with anger, though the general in charge turned out to be so refined and courteous it wasn't long before he and Mama were on the best of terms. In some ways it was similar to the time when I had polio and Mama had something to think about other than Papa and her grief. She became more sociable and began to take greater account of what was going on around her.

Mama was rather attractive and as a young widow with three daughters – Nanuck was at school in Florence – she had a special appeal many men found charming. But she was a lady, the German was a gentleman, and their friendship was confined to music, philosophy and poetry reading. Had there been more, I feel certain Mama's madness would never have surfaced, my own formative years would have been more disciplined and my whole life might have followed a different course. But then, for everyone life is a cluster of ifs and buts, and what *is* matters far more than what might have been.

Our greatest suffering during the German occupation was the indignity of being moved into the servants' quarters, though the general made up for it by devoting more energy to us than he did to the needs of his regiment. There was always a good supply of fresh food. He punished his men when they had the nerve to paint Christmas trees on the seventeenth-century white stucco walls of the house, and he made certain that the parcels Mama sent to her brother got through to the prison camp where he was being held. The general must have felt an empathy with Uncle Giulio's anti-Nazi stance. He was one of the group caught in the plot to assassinate Hitler, and was executed.

One of the new rules made at this time was that we were forbidden to talk to the soldiers. Naturally, I didn't take any notice, and naturally, Lorian always managed to find out. It happened with about the same regularity as the funeral bell that chimed through San Trovaso. In the end, I got so fed up with being punished I decided to seek revenge.

The next time a young man came to spend the evening with Lorian, I took six of those famous laxative pills, crushed them and put the powder in their drinks. They were running to the bathroom for days. I lived in fear of my life but it was worth it. It was the most daring thing I ever did.

I was growing up. The day-to-day affairs of the household had slipped into a routine and, as soon as they did, everything changed again.

It begun with the sad news that Nanuck's godfather, Amedeo d'Aosta, had died in a British prison camp. He was one of the last links to Papa, and his death cast Mama into a fresh state of despondency. She would have got through it but then, after we'd become accustomed to the presence of the Germans, they suddenly left and we were 'liberated' by the Americans. They too moved into the house. Mama was petrified and took to carrying a revolver that she had kept hidden for years.

During the German occupation lots of the village girls had been courted and sometimes molested by the pretty German boys, but when the 'Yanks' appeared it was a different matter. For one thing, some of them were black, and my mother, after her trips to Africa, had it in her mind that black people had greater and more uncontrollable urges. She and the general spoke the same language; the newcomers, with their wide grins and clumsy good manners, could have been invaders from another planet. She studied the faces, kept a firm grip on her gun and decided that, if anything disagreeable happened, she was going to shoot her three daughters and then shoot herself. I was taken aside daily and spoken to sternly.

'I have been very lenient with you for a very long time, Afdera,' Mama would say. 'But now I am serious. If I catch you speaking to any of these men you'll be in real trouble.'

'Yes, Mama.'

'You do understand?'

'Yes, Mama.'

I didn't, not fully, and Mama never made her true apprehensions clear. It was all part of the mystery that was men: something we didn't talk about but hummed over, like the bees around the flower beds.

I did speak to the American soldiers, though only when I knew I would get away with it. Neither I nor my sisters were interfered with and, if you pass through San Trovaso today, you won't find a coffee-coloured population but a faint legacy of blue eyes, blond hair and chiselled cheekbones. The Americans, so often and so much maligned, were as gentlemanly as our general.

The first American my mother got to know or wanted to know was Henry Fonda.

It is at this point that I have chosen to make these few reflections on my childhood because it was now, at the time of my mother's death, that I wandered back through the same little forest of memories and found that, among them, two other deaths stood out like signposts: when I saw the dead nun at the Sacred Heart Convent I reacted by planning never to grow up and never to grow old; and, when Simba died and I was barely twenty, I kept my heartache submerged in my secret box and retreated once more into immaturity.

Seven years had gone by and Mama's death came at a moment when

I had already decided to grow up and to make some great changes in my life. My marriage was a safety net and I knew I had to cut the strings and walk out alone if I was going to find myself. It was the right time for moving on – though not before I finally did something practical, and for others.

I arrived back in New York after the funeral, feeling guilty because I had been so inattentive to my mother and her desires. I was also haunted by the Memorial Hospital, and it was there one morning that I presented myself to a big, burly matron and volunteered to train as a nurse's aide, a job not dissimilar to that of an under-maid in a large house. You do only the worst, most unimaginable tasks – cleaning bed pans, inserting enemas and, the thing I despised, making beds. Ten enemas were better than making one bed. There were so many different ways of doing it, depending, among other things, on whether the patient was going into surgery or coming out of surgery, and I was always getting it wrong.

But I did it. First came the classes. It was like going to school, sitting in a classroom at a desk and learning all about the human body and how it showed signs of needing attention. Then there was a training period on the wards, and eventually I got my certificate.

Most of the people I knew were used to my frivolous nature and at first they thought the whole thing was a tremendous joke. 'I pity the poor patients,' said Peter Ustinov. 'I'll eat my cravat if she finishes the course,' promised David Niven. 'I'm going to check into the hospital and see this for myself,' laughed Renaldito Herrera. Fonda raised his eyebrows and, though he didn't say anything, he was really very pleased. He had been waiting for nearly four years for me to do something.

I got up early every morning, sometimes after the most spectacular functions, and not only did I finish the course and start work at Lenox Hill Hospital, I went for a further period of training that would allow me to go to Memorial.

The work wasn't any harder but, since it was a cancer hospital, I was continually subjected to the most pitiable forms of suffering. Before, whenever I had to face something unpleasant, I would just turn my back and walk away. Now, I couldn't. For once, there were others who were relying on me. It was an odd feeling, and a nice one. I surprised my friends and, in some ways, I surprised myself. There was nothing that I found horrifying – bed pans, the sight of blood, people dying. They were all natural; even death is a part of life.

Of course I had no intention of completely changing my personality and rather enjoyed some of the lighter things, like my uniform. It was off-white with a minute, pointless but very attractive hat and a blue elastic belt that was worn high and made your waist extremely tiny. I always took a bath in Arpège oil before I went on duty, which gave me a divine smell and pleased the patients. They all appeared to like me. I was relaxed, I didn't fuss over anyone and I showed I was human by making mistakes, particularly with the beds.

Eventually I chose to work exclusively in the children's ward, which I thought would be easy, though in fact the opposite was true. Adults with cancer are often peaceful and quiescent, as if the disease has given them fresh insights into the meaning of it all. Children, however, are angry and distressed, and seem to know that they won't get better. The hospital is usually the last battleground.

One little boy I remember was named Thomas. He was about six or seven, he had no hair, his body was covered in sores and he looked dreadful. For some reason he took to me and constantly asked for the nurse with the 'nice smell'. I was kind to him, I gave him lots of massages and, in the end, he gave me all his love and simply loathed his elderly adoptive mother and father – it was a sad and difficult situation.

As the months went by he became so attached to me that he started to scream at his parents when they so much as entered the ward. Each day they appeared greyer, smaller and older, and I felt more sorrow for them than I did for my patient. A couple of times when he cried for me in the night, the hospital telephoned and I dashed by taxi to his bedside. 'You don't want to start this,' Fonda said, but I went because I wanted to go. On the last occasion, I walked in and my heart jumped into my throat. Tommy had become a frightened, cornered animal. He looked sad and desperate, a poor little mite alone before the great darkness. I sat next to him. He gave me a faint smile, he held my hand, and then he died.

I remained where I was for a long time, not bottling up my feelings but finally releasing them in a lake of tears.

Eventually I took a taxi home. I lay in bed and stared at the ceiling. I was a woman, like many women, in a marriage that hadn't gone bad but had run its course. We had shared a vision, a private dream, and, lying there awake, I felt as if I had woken up. I was contaminated by all the reading I had done as a child. From it I had learned that freedom was a far greater friend than safety – at least that's what I thought then. I knew that people less privileged than I were trapped in marriage, for without it where else could they go? But I was privileged. I couldn't help that – but I could help myself. Fonda and I didn't argue, we didn't fight, we didn't do anything. We tolerated each other, like two strangers forced to share the same carriage on a train. I closed my eyes and saw the kite drifting untethered on the wind. I wanted to be the kite. Mama had died and my marriage, I had begun to realize, was probably dying.

The very next day I told Hank that I needed to get away for a while; he suggested that we have a trial separation, 'just to see what happens'.

It was a compromise and the best thing for us both. We went to the bank. Fonda gave me a cheque book, some traveller's cheques, and showed me where to sign and what to do. It was the first time I'd had an account of my own. We bought a round-trip ticket to Rome with a stopover in London and, a few days later, we were standing together at the departure gate at New York airport. Fonda's eyes were full of understanding.

'You're just a pony that has to go,' he said. 'But you'll come back to the stable.'

I smiled. Tears trickled on to my cheeks. I watched him as he walked away. He had a special way of walking and from the back he looked slightly stooped – it made me want to run after him and try all over again. But I didn't. I was a woman with boundless curiosity, whereas Hank was a man who had satisfied his. I had to go. Perhaps something was waiting for me out there in the world? I had a feeling, an intuition, something beyond words – perhaps the clouds the fortune teller had seen were just forming – perhaps Cancer was in conjunction with Venus? I knew deep down there was something.

9 . Ink

On the plane from New York, I sat next to an old friend, a bright young businessman named Mario Durso, who always reminds me of the Scarlet Pimpernel – here, there and everywhere. Our ceaseless chatter made the long flight seem shorter than usual.

It was Ascot week when I arrived in London. The early summer weather was glorious and I fell in love with England. The room I had at the Ritz was usually given to people like the Aga Khan's secretary; it was charming. It was in the attic and had a sloping ceiling and a view over a chessboard of red and grey rooftops. I could see a whole army of impressive buildings I didn't know and around them and everywhere were large islands of greenery. The city was far richer in parklands than Rome or New York. It was 1961 and really rather a good time to be in London. It was about to explode with the Beatles, with Mary Quant and mini-skirts, new ideas, new fashions, new film-makers, marvellous stage plays. The air was fresh and alive. I felt relieved to have my independence and thankful to have friends to take me under their wing. I was free – but not alone.

When I arrived, publisher George Weidenfeld acted like a mother hen and it was with him on one of the first evenings that I went to a ball organized by Kitty Miller, a resourceful lady and a renowned hostess who held the event annually, just like her spendid New Year's Eve parties in New York. It was an occasion for dressing up. Even if out on the streets the hemlines would soon be lifting, Kitty Miller's parties were deep in establishment territory; the men would be in dark suits and the ladies would be in their finest of finery. I had exactly the right thing: a Valentino dress, cut to leave one shoulder bare, in a material that shimmered between blue and green. I had long ear-rings and high, high heels – shoes that turned out, as usual, to be too tight. Almost as soon as I got there I was dying to slip them off, but it was one of those functions where you couldn't. I was at my best but it was a new environment. I felt just a little nervous, and pleaded with George not to leave me alone.

'No, of course not,' he said, and immediately disappeared.

The music was playing and couples twirled on the dance floor. I stood motionless for a long time and then, quite suddenly I had a funny feeling that someone was staring at me. I slowly turned and focused on a small, dark man who was leaning against a column. He had a large nose and eyes that peered out from sockets that were as deep and as dark as wells. He had a large head and large hands, all out of proportion, as if he should have been tall and wasn't. He ambled over to join me and, when he smiled, his whole face lit up.

'Would you like to dance?' he asked.

'Yes,' I said, without any hesitation.

He was short and I was a giant in my four-inch heels, but somehow we fitted together like two pieces of a puzzle, pieces that would fit in no other position. We danced as if we had been rehearsing. The man danced like a Latin – but quietly, without a gushing stream of Latin charm.

The band stopped playing and then started again and we continued to move around the floor. I was astonished that we danced so well together, and I was equally astonished by the man's smell, not Dunhill or anything like that, but something quite unique. Because of our different heights my nose was just above the top of his head, the aroma was wafting up, and, finally, I recognized what it was. It was ink – and not at all unpleasant. Ink!

He held me tight, we moved in unison. I felt odd. I felt as if I had known this man all my life, and the feeling terrified me. Love at first sight? Certainly not. It was chemistry at first touch, and it was something that had never ever happened before.

When the dance came to an end, I was glad to be able to run away and find safe, cosy George.

'Do you know the man you were dancing with?' he asked.

'No, I've never seen him before. Who is he?'

'Harry Cubitt. He's in the building business. I'm a close friend of his wife.'

I was none the wiser. The evening passed, and it was such a relief when I was back in my attic room at the Ritz and I could take my shoes off. I slipped between the clean crisp bedsheets, closed my eyes and tried to sleep. I couldn't. Butterflies were flying wildly in my stomach, and the smell of ink was everywhere.

Later that week I got a call from an old friend, the businessman David Metcalfe. He was married to Alexa, the widow of the legendary producer Alex Korda. Their little girl, Zara, was being christened on the Thursday. Following the ceremony, they were holding a small dinner party and I was invited.

'I d-d-d-don't th-th-think you'll kn-know anyone but it sh-sh-should be ra-ra-rather pleasant,' David said. He is well known for his stammer.

I was delighted to accept. Thursday came and I duly arrived.

I walked into the drawing room and the first person I saw was my dancing partner. I can't say that I had the surprise of my life because I didn't. He was there as if he was meant to be there. He was sitting in the bay window, one smart trouser leg crossed over the other. I could see his large hands and, for the first time, I saw his shoes. They were long, they were very well made, and they reminded me of the shoes my grandfather always wore. The man stood and David Metcalfe introduced us.

'Th-this is H-H-Harry Cu-Cu-Cubitt ... h-h-have you m-met Af-Af-Afdera F-F-Fonda?'

We stood there, waiting patiently, and when David left to look after his other guests Harry and I began talking as if we were already in the middle of a conversation, one of those conversations friends pick up and put down again for years. I have been told that I am not a good listener, but with this man I listened carefully because he had such a beautiful voice and because everything he said somehow connected with everything I was thinking and was about to say myself. It was uncanny.

After a while, we got round to all the typical things. I told him that I was spending some time on my own to try out my marriage and he told me that his wife was away on holiday. It was all very matter of fact, without undercurrents or hidden meanings. We had an instant rapport, we liked each other, and our common sense told us that there was no more to it than that.

The dinner came and went. Once more we began talking and, for a moment, David came to join us.

'What t-time should we arrive to-morrow?' he asked Harry.

'About six, David, if that's all right with you.'

'Pppppperfect.'

Then he turned to me: 'What are you doing for the weekend?'

'I'm not sure. I'll probably go to the theatre. I haven't made any plans.' At that particular time I was busy running around seeing all the plays, going to galleries: my new independence was nothing if not energizing.

'Well, why don't you come too?' Harry now said. 'I have a little cottage. The Metcalfes are coming with a few others.'

'Fine, absolutely. It sounds wonderful.'

The cottage turned out to be *molto tipico*: wooden beams, a thatched roof and tiny windows like shiny crystal eyes. Outside there was a watermill, a pond, tall trees, English green meadows and a blue English sky. It was a picture straight from a postcard; the only thing out of place was a small swimming pool that was hidden in the garden.

'This is our bogus caricature of an English cottage,' Harry said the second I arrived.

'It's charming,' I replied.

'In a very bogus sort of way.' He was a man who underplayed his hand.

I admired the garden, I wandered inside the cottage and, as I did so, a man materialized from the kitchen with a tray loaded down with drinks. Now I did have the surprise of my life: the man was a perfect replica of Giuseppe. I went upstairs. In those days, even in cottages someone always came to unpack the luggage, and who was it? – a carbon copy of Fidalma. The coincidence was remarkable, and it made me feel most at home. Harry's couple were named Alide and Adriana and they were as close to him as Fidalma and Giuseppe were to me.

During the evening, while the other guests were talking, Harry invited me to join him for a swim. It was very strange to swim – and in England! But the weather was unusually warm and so I said yes. We changed, we jumped in, we swam around for a while and then we paddled with our heads above the water and continued our ceaseless conversation. I don't know how we found so much to talk about but we did. There was nothing odd about that, of course, but what was extraordinary was that, at the exact same second, two sets of teeth began chattering away like tom-toms and we both leapt out of the pool and rushed to get changed. It was as if we were a pair of marionettes joined by the same set of strings.

Throughout the weekend we exchanged long looks but we didn't touch each other. On the contrary, we actually made a point of not going anywhere near each other.

When David Metcalfe drove me back to London on Sunday, I asked him if I should write a thank-you letter.

'It's not the sort of thing I normally do,' I said.

'Then don't b-bother,' he stammered. 'I'll tell the L-l-l-little M-m-man for you.'

It was David's name and it stuck. Harry became the Little Man.

I was leaving for Rome the following weekend. On the Wednesday, he called.

'Can I come and see you at tea-time at the Ritz?' he said.

'Why yes, of course you can come and see me at tea-time at the Ritz,' I replied.

I had been thinking about him all of the time, and he had been thinking about me; and we both made sure we didn't show it. There was a very special and tidy look about him. He always had nice suits; this one was topped off with a bowler hat, a briefcase and an umbrella. We talked, only our words didn't gush out quite as quickly as before. We were afraid to say what we wanted to say and, finally, we parted without making any arrangements to meet again. Somehow, we didn't need to.

I left London for Italy, I joined a party of people on Annibale's yacht and we set off round the Mediterranean. It was like being a girl again. Annibale knew that my marriage to Fonda was on the rocks. He paid me plenty of attention but I didn't respond. My mind was elsewhere. I kept to myself, I spent a lot of time relaxing in the sun. I even joined in the newest craze and went topless, something I wouldn't have done a year earlier.

I was really preoccupied by the present, though the voyage did make me think back for a moment to the previous summer. Hank and I had cruised the Aegean on Peter Ustinov's boat, the *Nitchevo*, a slow journey over a calm and windless sea until a freak storm appeared from nowhere and thrust us into the most awful danger. We were suddenly in a grey wall of water, the horizon tilting back and forth like a seesaw: Peter's wife Suzanne and I huddled together in the cabin like two drowning rats.

We wept, we prayed, we were rocked from side to side. It went on for so long, I eventually plucked up my courage and slowly climbed the cabin steps. The sky was black, the wind was howling like a wounded monster; Hank and Peter were two yellow ghosts wavering in the distance; and hanging on to a rope just above my head was one of the crewmen.

'Are we sinking?' I shouted in Italian.

'Yes, we are,' he yelled back in Spanish. 'In Mykonos.'

It was very funny – though not at the time. I thought we really *were* sinking.

The waters were calm on this cruise. Each day on Annibale's yacht the sun rose earlier and the temperature rose higher. I ate lots of fish and felt lean and healthy. We visited Lorian at her summer house and, as we sailed from the Isola del Giglio that morning, I happened to glance out to sea as a small motor boat was cruising into the harbour. I gasped. There was the Little Man. Our eyes met. He jumped up. I jumped up and we both waved frantically. He was going in as I was going out. It was something that had to be. Harry's wife was also there, like a shadow in the background.

I had many confused thoughts and it is difficult to describe now, after so many years, the feelings I had during those first encounters. Similarly, it is hard to put those feelings into perspective among other things that were more important. Everyone can remember what they were doing the moment they were told that Jack Kennedy had been shot. Incidents one can recall, but feelings are much more elusive.

Meeting Harry in England and then seeing him from Annibale's boat was quite odd, but it was only one part of what was turning out to be a very intense period for me in Italy during my trial separation. I was full of moods and conflicts within myself. I loved being back with old friends like Annibale, but it was not with them that I was going to find the answer to what I was going to do during the next few years of my life.

San Trovaso was the place I was missing most. The house had always been there to welcome me with open arms. It was like a harbour where I felt protected. But it had all changed. I missed my crazy, eccentric Mama and the old servants. They had been part of the family and they had all gone. My sister-in-law Kristina had taken over. The atmosphere was different and it was no longer my home.

I had lost my home but, thank God, one thing I had always had and still have is my friends. Having close relationships came to me instinctively. Like my father, who was an explorer of places, I have always been an explorer of people, people from every different part of the world and from every sort of background. The young actors and directors and writers I met when I joined the theatre when I first left home have remained close always and, even if I don't see those people for a long time, when I do see them we pick up exactly where we left off.

One of those special people from the early days was Beatrice Monti, now married to the great novelist Gregor von Rezzori. During those years, she had discovered an enchanting village on the island of Rhodes called Lindos. She had a gallery in Milan and her house on the island had become a sort of commune for artists from all over the world. Her companion then was the sculptor Andrea Cascella, who looked like one of his own statues – rough, sharp-angled and in the finest quality stone.

Beatrice allowed people to get on with their own thing and, through her, many artists were to flourish. She helped launch the painters Rothko and de Kooning and many others in Europe, and was one of the first, if not the first, to recognize the genius of the Italian painter Tancredi, who committed suicide in the 1970s. Another supporter of Tancredi and the arts in general is my cousin Giorgio Franchetti, whose apartment in Rome is more like a gallery than a home. It's full of the most marvellous things.

I went to stay with Beatrice that summer for three weeks and it was pure heaven. I was away from it all and was able to think my own thoughts among new people, people who didn't love me or criticize me but accepted me the way I was.

The way of life was primitive. I slept on the roof of the house. Everyone went to bed early and got up early. I read; Andrea worked on his sculpture on the terrace. We went out in a small boat and we caught fish to cook for lunch. Everything was real and serene and, if you had problems, the mood was right for you to be able to think them through. I had worked through a few ideas. I had definitely decided to leave Fonda; Harry was in the back of my mind; and I had another plan. A photographer came from *Vogue* to take photographs of Beatrice's house and I wondered what it would be like to take a job on the magazine. I like travelling, I liked meeting people. It seemed like an ideal occupation.

When I left Lindos I went to see Lorian. The gap that had always existed between us, something beyond the ten years that separated our ages, had somehow broadened and yet, at the same time, become more difficult to define. Something was wrong, but I didn't know what.

In Rome there were lots of letters for me from Hank and, when I arrived in Venice, he called by telephone with the news that his son Peter was getting married and that the house was to be used for the reception.

'If you haven't decided to return yet, you obviously don't want to stay with me,' he said.

'Hank, I . . .'

'Either you come back now, as my wife, or don't come back at all.'

I hated ultimatums.

'I need to be on my own still, Hank, I'm sorry.'

He didn't reply and the conversation ended inconclusively. I stayed away until after Peter's wedding, to be fair to Peter, and returned a few days later. Hank was at the airport to meet me, with a present, a crystal leaf from Tiffany's which he had bought at the suggestion of Jack Kennedy's sister, Pat Lawford. 'If you really want her back,' she said, 'take a little gift.' I opened the box, but it was not something that was going to solve the problem.

'Hank, I want to be independent, I need my freedom,' I explained.

He listened, although he didn't listen. He went off to California to make another film, *Advise and Consent*, and everything was left in the air. We spent Christmas together at the house with the journalist Furio Colombo and the painter Brian Stonehouse, two good friends of ours, then Hank rushed back to Hollywood before I had the chance to sit him down with a lawyer and a set of divorce papers.

The weather in New York was bleak and cold, I wasn't exactly sure what to do next, which made Sibilla O'Donnell's voice over the telephone one morning a more than pleasant surprise. We had known each other forever. Like me she was an Italian, a Tormacelli, originally from Naples. We hadn't seen each other for a while and so she invited me to visit her in the sunshine of Nassau.

'Why don't you come and stay?' she said. 'There's a wedding next week, I'm sure you'll love it.'

I wasn't so sure: I always weep at weddings.

'Mmm,' I replied.

'John Wilton and Diana Neylan-Leyland are taking the plunge,'

Sibilla continued. 'I don't know if you know the best man, his name's Harry Cubitt.'

'Don't worry, I'll come ...' I agreed quickly.

I was on the next plane to the Bahamas.

I remained quietly in the corner. I watched the Little Man and he watched me. I returned home, he arranged a business meeting in New York, and then he came to find me. We looked, we talked. I was frightened, but when we made love it was as if we had known each other since the beginning of time. We didn't fall madly in love at that second; love doesn't last if it comes too easily. It has to come slowly, and that was how it happened for me.

We were testing ourselves and each other, in case our feelings were born in the land of illusion. It was like a dream, but a waking dream.

We went to the park and stamped over the frosty grass and the memories that flooded back to me were so distant they didn't matter. I was so happy to be with Harry; the past had crumbled away and need never have existed. We went out to ride on one of the little boats. But when we looked at each other closely, what we saw was a future filled with clouds. I wish I had reached out, then, in that very second and never ever let go. Only one great love comes in each lifetime. It is as unique and as singular as birth and death. When it comes, we must recognize it and instantly hold on tight. Harry and I recognized it and it scared us to death. He was married. I was still married. There were conventions to observe, decency, loyalty, habit. There were other people to consider and we did consider them. It was the most foolish thing we could have done. The relationship was so intense and dramatic and all so quick that, with the drawing of its first breath, the seeds of doom had also been sown.

Harry started a business in Montreal. Each time he flew back to England, I missed him terribly: our only contact was the telephone call at precisely eleven every morning. We talked and talked and talked. When the Beatles arrived in America I described the commotion at the airport, when the Cuban exiles landed in the Bay of Pigs we discussed that – it didn't matter what we talked about as long as I heard his voice.

Harry and I were kept apart by circumstances and convention. Harry was still caught between loyalty to his wife, who had helped him through a very difficult period of his life, and his love for me. And I was still Mrs Henry Fonda.

As the months of 1962 fell away, my life alternated between the joy of the odd seconds I spent with Harry and the tension I felt extinguishing the last glimmers of light in my marriage. I told Fonda many times that I wanted a divorce but he didn't seem to take it seriously until Lil Groueff went to see him and made it clear on my behalf. Lil and her husband Stephane, the New York editor of *Paris Match*, had decided to be kind and protective towards me, though they were also close to Hank, and it was at their house in Southampton, Long Island, that Harry and I sometimes stayed. At first, Lil had thought I was crazy wanting a divorce.

'It's only a moment of crisis. It will pass,' she told me.

Stephane Groueff was more philosophical. 'I can understand,' he said. 'You'll start again.'

Another friend who helped at that time was Elsie Woodward: 'Don't get a divorce until you're damned sure you've got someone else,' she said. She was ruthless and marvellous. Elsie was a famous socialite – not that that does her justice. She was one of the most fascinating and powerful women I ever met.

I didn't mind listening to advice, but my mind was already made up. Fonda finally bought me the flat I carefully chose on Park Avenue so that I would have somewhere to live. We divided our possessions, and I arranged to fly to Juárez in Mexico, where the divorce procedure was very straightforward. Everything was set. It was my last night at East 74th, Fonda was staying at an hotel. At four in the morning, the telephone rang.

'You can still change your mind, you know, even now,' he said. His voice was blurred by alcohol and it didn't sound like him at all.

'Darling, I know I'm making the biggest mistake of my life but I must go through with it.'

He put the phone down. It was one of the few times that I called my husband darling.

The kite was free. I had made the final break.

In Mexico, there were four other women also waiting to see the judge and annul their marriages. One was nine months pregnant, one was crying, one was knitting, and the fourth stared at me from the second I arrived. I was the last to go in. I was tired from a sleepless night and was tense because of the fear I still suffered every time I boarded an aeroplane. In truth I was also still in a state of indecision.

'Do you hate your husband?' the judge inquired.

'No.'

'Is he cruel?'

'No.'

'Is he impotent? Is it because the ages are wrong? Is he unkind?'

'No, no, no, he's a lovely man.'

'Then why do you want to end this marriage?'

I remembered that Susan Blanchard had been vicious when it had come to her divorce and I didn't want to be the same. I had nothing against Hank and I had no intention of making anything up.

'I don't know why, I just do,' I then answered. 'I'm too immature. I want to be on my own.'

The judge looked like a very wise old crow as he nodded his head slowly back and forth.

'Do you feel that your characters are incompatible?' he asked very solemnly.

Yes, I thought – but not always. There were times when everything was quite perfect. The previous summer we had been to stay with the Italian film producer Marina Cicogna and her mother, the Countess Anna Maria Cicogna, at their home on the Libyan coast, a house later taken over and converted into a fortress by Colonel Gaddafi. The heavy, warm air acted like an aphrodisiac. Hank read poetry from the steps of a ruined amphitheatre. We spent nearly every moment alone together and we were anything but incompatible. Timing was the essence. In those final weeks, while every day Hank had the regrets over another failed marriage to think about, each night he was going out on stage on Broadway to play a man dying of cancer. There was irony in the coincidence, though his reviews were among the best he ever had.

All these thoughts moved through my tired mind and the words that came out were said in all honesty.

'We are slightly incompatible,' I murmured.

The judge continued to nod. He scribbled over the form on his desk. He signed, I signed. It was done.

We were now in the last days of 1962. I returned alone to my flat in New York. I was truly in love for the first time and I was going through the suffering once defined by Gloria Stewart: I was suffering for love. It was a slow process: a voice gradually emptying of laughter; a day when the telephone didn't ring; a long conversation that dried into small deserts of silence. Things were not going well with Harry. It became upsetting; then there was nothing for me to do but not allow it to upset me. I was a free spirit and I had to try out the wings of my freedom. I rented my apartment to the Hungarian producer we all called Johnny Goulash. I told Harry I was going away, and then disappeared, visiting friends, wandering; where I can't remember; though my return three months later is far less forgettable.

While I was away, Warren Beatty had gone to see the Hungarian on several occasions and had become haunted by the portrait of me in the drawing-room. In his own way, he fell in love with me in oils and was determined to bring the painting to life. Harry was always in the back of my mind, but Warren was young, talented, amusing – and there. We began to see each other, and it was fun. I was laughing again. He was completely in touch with the moment and I followed his lead. I lived in the present and shrugged away each little feeling of guilt as it appeared. Harry knew I loved him and, because I loved him, I wanted to hurt him.

For Warren and me it was just a fling, short and sweet, not that the brevity stopped the gossip from racing across the Atlantic to Harry.

Everything that he was told was terribly exaggerated. In public, we were the most demure couple in the world, and in private Warren Beatty was simply fun to be with. He smelled of honey and like Lady Chatterley with her lover, he was the sort of man whose body you wanted to cover in daisy chains. He was naughty, charming and playful, spraying me with a soda siphon one minute and talking seriously the next. He spent a lot of time in front of the mirror. He thought he was much too beautiful and was dying to have grey hair and wrinkles. He also had a complex over his sister Shirley MacLaine.

'Shirley's got character in her face,' he would say. 'I'm not at all interesting.'

He wasn't even being modest. He *was* good-looking – and he found it a bore.

He was like a shadow in the night: he came and he went. We parted amicably and the next time I saw him was almost two years later at an airport with Leslie Caron; he was arriving and I was departing.

'Hello. You look marvellous,' I said.

'Hi, there, so do you,' he replied.

Warren Beatty was for me an enjoyable interlude, and I can see why women have fallen in love with him.

134

I missed my eleven o'clock calls from Harry. So much was happening – Khrushchev in New York, Fidel Castro, Pope John – all things I wanted to talk about – but only with Harry. Love was the key that had opened the door to new dimensions of feeling, new extremes. It was like being plunged into icy water. I was completely and totally alive. Harry was giving his marriage a second go – not that you can reheat a cold plate – and I had no desire to replace him.

I had been thinking about trying to get a job with American *Vogue* since the previous summer when I was at Lindos, and now I finally put my plan into action. I knew some of the people there, I offered my services and, after a little reluctance, I was employed on a trial basis. Diana Vreeland, the editor, saw me as having 'potential', and someone else must have thought that I was some sort of expert on shopping. At any rate, I was put in charge of a column called 'Shop Hound'. I was supplied with a secretary, a Mexican girl named Maria Pierre Colle, who, fortunately, had exactly the same accent as I and who covered for me when I should have been in the office or during the times when I was having a snooze.

Before I began on the magazine, 'Shop Hound' had always been full of the most boring things, like where to buy fancy toilet paper, raffia baskets and chain saws. I wanted to inject some life into it and quickly added items of exotica like rare cats and parakeets. Naturally I brought my wildlife back to the office to be photographed and, once things were there, they tended to remain.

'There isn't even enough space for us to hang our coats,' groaned the head of fashion Grace Mirabella. 'And as soon as we try to take a photograph, one of Mrs Fonda's parrots flies in to bombard us.'

My animals were annoying the models and making the most undesirable additions to the patterns created by Valentino, Givenchy, Balenciaga. 'It's like working in a zoo,' Grace observed, and she was right. It had become so bad there was nothing they could do except promote me.

I was moved upstairs to the features department, without Maria Pierre, but to a huge office that I shared with Pamela Colin, a serious career girl who later married David Harlech, the English peer who for years was the head of the film censorship board. Then from out of the blue one morning Harry phoned and the long conversation started as if it had never been left off.

Now it was my long conversations, rather than my animals, that became a problem.

'I wouldn't mind but they are usually fascinating and I can't get any work done because I'm too busy listening,' Pamela complained.

Diana Vreeland was most understanding. She thought it over for a long time and then reached the same decision she had made before. 'Well, she does have potential, we don't want to lose her.'

I was promoted again, to overseas feature writer, and shipped to Venice to meet the highly-respected photographer Ugo Mulas, who was anything but dying to meet me.

'What are you doing sending me a socialite butterfly from New York?' He reproached art director Alex Lieberman.

'See how it goes. If she's no good, we'll send someone else,' Mulas was told.

The photographer ground his teeth and waited. I flew to Rome and then took the train to Venice. It was like arriving in my own city as a tourist. The train was completely empty – not a soul. I stepped out at eight in the morning, wandered along the platform, and there was Mulas, pale, grey hair over a strained young face, and an expression that didn't say welcome. But I gave him such a great big smile that he had to smile back. I had a nice feeling for him and he immediately responded. We became friends.

'I'm told you never move before noon,' were his opening words.

'Not very often,' I admitted.

He glanced at his watch. 'Well, I've got you up now. We're not going to waste a second.'

We left my luggage at the Bauer, one of the newest hotels in the city, and no less appealing even through the mid-sixties, when the ground-floor furniture and carpets had to be taken up every time there was a high tide. Like everything in Venice, it brought back endless memories. Tortorella, the hotel's fabled custodian, was a man with a heart of gold and the incredible gift of being able to arrange *anything*. Once when Simba collapsed and went into a coma, Tortorella managed to have another train delayed so that the train carrying my sister was able to go from Cortina to Florence without stopping. An amazing man. He was there in the foyer. We chatted away for a few minutes, my cases were collected by a porter, and I set off with Mulas.

As always, Venice touched all my emotions. I felt happy, sad, nostalgic, at home, drawn back by the umbilical cord that had been there since the day I was born. Everything was as familiar as my own skin: the canals, the bridges, the stone buildings rising up like windows into the past – my own past as well as all the centuries before my existence. We passed the small cinema where I used to sit holding hands with Marino de la Garda, over the back of the seats because Baroness Stockhausen, our chaperone, would plonk herself down like a rock between us. We went to the island of San Giorgio and to the Lido, where I looked out across the beach half expecting to see the ice-cream seller from my childhood, the flags, the family bathing hut adorned with a large letter 'F' and another next door with a 'C' for the Cicognas. Both were gone. It was February and the sands were deserted except for a single figure, a man bent against the lagoon winds walking a pair of dogs.

The day passed quickly, and I was so stimulated by the company of Ugo Mulas and so adored him that I soon set up another feature for us to cover in Rome, a portrait study of various Romans that would include Luchino Visconti, Prince and Princess Aspreno Colonna with their three children, my sister Lorian with her six children, and the young painter Mario Schifano, a man who was later to play a key role in my life's most extraordinary drama.

During those winter days at the beginning of 1963 I felt that my job with *Vogue* was turning out to be better than I had ever expected. Part of that was simply due to Mulas, a talented photographer but, more, a very special man. He was suffering from an incurable disease that made him appear much older than he was. He knew that he didn't have very long to live and, as he had told me on the platform at Venice station, he didn't want to waste a moment. Everything about him was fast and urgent – his work, his words, his mind. He thought he was getting a New York socialite to work with him and was pleased to find that he was wrong. I was still a part of that world but I had now begun to open my eyes to other worlds as well.

One evening when we were having dinner, I told him about my grandfather's funeral.

When Grandma Moceniga Mocenigo died, her husband, Grandpa Mario Rocca, moved to a little palace to live with a woman we called Spritze, the name given to the drink made up from half white wine and half soda. She was Austrian or German and a baroness from some old, forgotten family.

She was Nonno Mario's companion for several years, but, when he died in 1950, she was ushered into the background by our family and even more so by four little men who appeared wearing masks and long cloaks on the day of the funeral. Only then did we discover that Mario Rocca was one of the Brothers of the Misericordia, a Catholic secret society that helps the poor. However wealthy an individual member of the Brotherhood is, when he dies he is buried in the same way as the poor people. Even the Brothers aren't supposed to know who among the members are rich and who aren't; but even though their faces and clothes are kept hidden, you can tell by looking at their shoes.

The four masked men carried a bare wooden coffin. Grandpa Rocca was placed inside and, without flowers or decoration, it was lowered into a small black gondola. It departed, the big hooked prow carving a slow path through the early morning mist; the family followed behind by motor boat. We sat quietly with our own thoughts. The canals were empty and the city streets were deserted. It was silent ... but then the silence was broken by the sound of hurrying footsteps. I glanced out as we were going under the Rialto Bridge and saw a figure keeping pace with the cortège. It was Spritze, all in black and with a long veil that hid her face. She followed for a long time and only came to a halt when she reached the last bridge and there she stood and watched as the gondola moved across the flat open sea towards the island cemetery where my grandfather was to be buried.

I stared back as her tiny black form grew smaller and then disappeared. Inside, I felt an overwhelming sadness for Spritze that completely overshadowed the sorrow I had over the death of my grandfather. She had obviously loved him, she had done no harm to anyone and I thought it was awful that she had been left behind. I am sure my mother would have agreed to her joining us, but Uncle Giulio, her brother, for all he had gone through during the war, was still very conservative.

We arrived at the island, the simple burial began, and, as I watched from under my hat, I began to wonder what would become of all Grandpa Rocca's shoes. He wore the very best English brogues, that he always cared for and cleaned himself. They were beautiful – and the same sort of shoes that Harry wore.

I finished my story and Ugo Mulas was so enthralled he decided that we should return to Venice to set up a fake funeral and photograph it for the magazine. It was our third feature and, as with the first two,

Diana Vreeland cabled back the critique, 'SENSATIONAL', though most of the ideas we had were really wrong for *Vogue*, with its emphasis on fashion and beauty.

There was also another problem. We spent small fortunes setting up our stories. They had put me on the staff thinking I was going to bring in some new blood and I just brought bills. Mulas was a freelance photographer and, as I was on the payroll, I was the one who had to go.

When I returned to New York everyone knew I was going to get the sack, although no one had the heart to tell me. Alex Lieberman, Ed Russell, who frequently took me out to dinner and was rumoured to be my lover, though he wasn't, and Pat Patsevich all avoided me when I was in the office, and it was finally left to Diana Vreeland to do the deed.

I was summoned one afternoon at four o'clock.

'Oh, well, I suppose I deserve it,' I told Maria Pierre; she and most of the girls wore amused faces.

Diana Vreeland sat back in her large leather chair looking like a carving in cork. There was a fresh anemone in a vase and the room smelled sweet from the perfumed candle that was burning in its holder on the desk.

'I've looked up your birth chart,' she said. She paused for a moment and then continued in hushed tones: 'You're a Cancer, your Ascendent is Leo and Saturn is moving into the most perfect conjunction.'

I stared back, speechless.

'You are so lucky, Afdera: it is the right time in your life to start something new.'

I was thrilled. Diana convinced me of my good fortune in leaving *Vogue* and I waltzed out of her room – much to the surprise of the girls. They had thought that I was going to be unhappy, but I wasn't. Nobody knew, but I had decided to quit the job before I lost it, and losing it made things easier for me.

Apart from sparking off my own interest in astrology, Diana Vreeland was a woman who fascinated me in many ways. When you first meet her you think: my God, what an ugly woman. After five minutes, you find her beautiful. You want to look like her, talk like her, be her. She has a special clean crispness about her. She adores beauty and beautiful things, beautiful people; she didn't care how much money she spent in making the pages of *Vogue* into mirror images of her own visions and ideas. In fact, it became so bad that in the end she, too, was fired – by Alex Lieberman, of all people.

By then she was already over seventy, but she still consumed a bottle of vodka a day and was as fit as a fiddle. She had no intention of sitting back in quiet retirement and, on the contrary, immediately set off on a world tour. The first leg of her journey took her to London, and by then lots of the reporters and editors who had worked for Diana had moved there themselves. I was one; there was Pamela Harlech, Robin Butler and several others.

I happened to remember that Diana loved anemones. They were not available in England at that moment but, with Harry's help, I managed to find a supply in Holland and duly sent a bouquet to the Ritz in time for Diana's arrival. I didn't think anyone else would have the same idea, but I couldn't have been more wrong. The day that Diana got to London, you couldn't move in or out of the hotel without stumbling over flowers.

'Mrs Vreeland, we have never had flowers like this,' said the head man. 'Even when kings and queens stayed here, even in the days of the Aga Khan. It's marvellous, unbelievable – but why?'

'Darling, they're for my funeral,' Diana replied.

By now, Diana Vreeland must be ninety, and she's still going strong. Sadly, Ugo Mulas died the year after we worked together in Italy. He was no more than forty.

10 . In the Cage

It was several years later, a late afternoon at the end of July, and the temperature was steadily rising in the long arrival hall at Rome airport. I was waiting for my luggage. I bought some magazines and glanced casually over the pages. First one; a second; a third. The minute hand on the large wall clock clicked through its arc: ten past, twenty past. I got up and peered through the glass partition that separated me from the main terminal. The friend who was due to meet me was nowhere to be seen. In a way it was a relief. It would only create more complications ...

I had flown to Rome from London, where I had been one of the guests at the marriage of George Weidenfeld and Sandra Payson. I had gone because years earlier George and I had made a promise that if either of us got married the other would drop whatever he was doing to attend. George's cable had found me sailing in Turkey. I was surprised that he had remembered our agreement, but the onus was on me to keep it. I had found a flight, first to Rome, on to London, and now, there I was, back again in the Italian capital – and waiting.

The other passengers had collected their bags and cases and the hall had slowly emptied of people. The room was silent except for the whir of the luggage conveyor. The mood was tense, expectant. I closed the last of my magazines and, as I did so, three men appeared at the other end of the hall and made their way towards me. One of them was in uniform, a policeman.

They stopped directly in front of me and one of the men not in uniform moved slightly ahead of the other two.

'Mrs Fonda?' he inquired.

'Yes. Why? What's happening?'

The man hesitated and then continued cautiously: 'I believe you may be carrying something?'

'I've got my bag and some magazines,' I said. 'My cases appear to have got lost.'

'Yes, yes, of course,' the man added. 'But don't you have something else?'

I had been sitting there in a haze of preoccupation. The same cycle of thoughts had been spinning through my mind for months, even years, and while I had been going over it all once again I had completely forgotten the parcel that had been brought to my hotel room in London. I stared at the man and his two companions: three short, dark men all vaguely similar to Giuseppe, one a policeman and the speaker clearly his boss. It was all beginning to make sense.

'You do have something else, don't you?' the same man repeated.

The room had become as hot as an oven. The mechanical luggage chute hummed in the distance. The question hung in the air, as ominous as a bird of prey.

'Yes, I do,' I finally answered. I nervously reached for my bag. I pulled out the small package and held it in my palm. 'I have this. It's some cigarettes – with marijuana.'

Once more there was a brief silence. The man (I was later to learn that he was the head of the Rome police) was on the trail of an entire drug ring and it was obvious by my attitude and the amount of contraband I carried that I wasn't a part of it. In the package there were three dope-filled, hand-rolled cigarettes, something far more stupid than dangerous and with a value of almost nothing.

The man took the little parcel and weighed it in his own palm. He shook his head and a faint smile creased his lips.

'You could have denied knowing what it was,' he said.

'Yes, but why? I do know,' I replied. 'Anyway, they're not mine. They're for a friend who's waiting outside for me.'

'I'm afraid your friend isn't outside, Mrs Fonda.'

'He's not? But ...'

'Mario Schifano has been arrested. He's awaiting trial in the Regina jail.'

The blood drained from my face. It had stopped being a joke. Mario in jail. I knew what was going on, but the Regina was like Sing Sing or Devil's Island, a dark, dangerous, notorious place that held the worst and most violent criminals. A decade or so later it would become known, not as Regina Coeli, but 'Chez Régine', because so many politicians, top people and good friends had been there. Then, it was like a very exclusive club, but not that baking July day in the nineteen sixties. It was hell. Mario was in jail. The words were a flashing neon sign inside my skull, something abstract, something I couldn't quite comprehend. Mario wasn't a criminal, but a painter, an artist, a free spirit. Jail, any confinement, would destroy him.

The concern I had for Mario was so powerful, it took many long seconds for me to trace his arrest back to my own predicament.

'But I have given you the package,' I then said in a hopeful voice. 'I'd like to go home now. I mean, I haven't done anything, have I?'

The police chief frowned and the tiny smile vanished from his mouth.

'Unfortunately, Mrs Fonda, it's not as simple as that,' he said.

The four of us stood there in the hot silence. I looked at each of the three men in turn and, involuntarily, I began to tremble. A great anxiety was welling up inside me – though not about my crime. It was as distant as the bombers that had once passed over San Trovaso. I knew that I would survive – but would the things that were important to me survive? Something had been building up in my life, something very special, very real. Suddenly it seemed so fragile.

'You'll have to come with us to the station and answer some questions,' the police chief was now saying. 'The possession of drugs is a serious offence.'

The uniformed policeman took my handbag and magazines. We moved away but, as we did so, I remembered the rest of my luggage and stopped to peer back at the empty conveyor belt.

'What about my things?' I said.

'We already have them,' the man replied.

We started up again. I followed the uniformed man the length of the arrival hall, out through a side door and then into the back of a waiting car. The police chief sat next to me and we pulled away. Dusk was falling but it was still very hot and the shimmering air made the car's reflection in the shop windows look like a mirage. I felt as if I were in a dream. I couldn't believe that what was happening could really be happening to me.

The dream image persisted when we reached the police headquarters. It could have been the set for a movie: the stained walls and crumbling brickwork, the high, echo-filled rooms all grimy with the patina of time and neglect. It was oppressive, it would have created feelings of guilt in the most innocent of people. I felt as if I had been taken to another country, another world, and I couldn't associate the ugly, dilapidated building with the Rome I knew – the squares, the galleries, the chic and colourful streets.

I was taken to a large room where an old-fashioned fan churned its way through air that was stale and dusty. A woman had been summoned from her home to search me and, when she arrived, the two of us went to a smaller room where I had to remove my clothes. The woman seemed embarrassed and tried to make conversation – about her three children, about her holidays that were about to begin. It was the weekend that takes July into August and the entire population was fleeing the city. She glanced away as I did my striptease. I was wearing a plain, sleeveless green dress, a pretty slip and bra, and I was tanned black from the Turkish sunshine.

When I was naked the woman went through my clothes and then, with eyes averted, she came and ran her hands over my body. It was supposed to be a thorough and intimate search but it wasn't. I dressed again, and when we returned to the large room the woman reported that I had nothing hidden, and then disappeared.

I was ushered into a third room, and there the dream started to become a nightmare. Photographs of me were taken from every angle and then the plain clothes policeman produced an ink pad and proceeded to take my fingerprints. I was horrified. I felt as if subtly, step by step, my very dignity was being devoured by the legal machine, by a cold, hard, uncaring bureaucracy. I felt numb. If someone had pushed a pin into me I wouldn't have felt a thing. I leaned over the ink pad, the smell drifted up into my consciousness and I could think of only one thing, one person: Harry. After everything we had been through we were ready to get back together once more; and now I was certain that I would never see him again.

We were supposed to be meeting a few days later at the Grand Hotel in Rome, where I had reserved a room. That was why I wasn't disappointed when Mario Schifano had failed to show up at the airport. Mario was a man who appealed to my dark side; he was the hand that reached out in the night and when he reached for me I went. I went in order to punish Harry but I always ended up punishing myself. It was Mario who had set up the delivery of the package at the Ritz in London –

one of his friends had come with both that and two LP records not then available in Italy. It was a recipe for disaster. I knew that if I met Schifano I would end up back at his studio and, in my own judgement, it would be an immoral thing to do – immoral, not because we might make love, but because I was in love with Harry.

The policeman gave me a cloth to wipe my fingers and, as he did so, the chief reappeared and sat on the desk between me and his colleague. I had already answered various questions, simple, regulation things – my name, my age, nothing dramatic. I had been charged with being in possession of marijuana and I thought that now, finally, I was going to be allowed to go.

'Well, Mrs Fonda, that's about it for tonight,' the chief said.

'That means I can leave. No?' I asked in a small, soft voice.

The man suddenly appeared grim and apologetic. 'I'm sorry, but I'm afraid it doesn't,' he said. 'We're going to have to take you to Rebibbia.' He paused; then, when he continued, the rest of his words came at me as if through a dense fog: '... the type of offence ... held until a date to be fixed ... all the evidence has been collected ...'.

'But it was only a mistake,' I broke in. 'I haven't done it before.'

The man shrugged and held out his two palms. 'I'm sorry, the law's the law. There's nothing I can do, even if I wanted to.'

I tried to say something else but the words got stuck in my throat and died. The man opposite pushed back his chair and, as if that was a signal, I stood, the chief left his place on the desk and the three of us shuffled out of the room, along the corridor and back to the car. Once more the chief of police sat next to me and, this time, he took my hand and held it with great tenderness. *Rebibbia*, I was thinking, *Rebibbia*. The women's jail was as infamous as the Regina Coeli, though still I was less concerned with the immediate misery of being incarcerated than I was by the awful consequences it was likely to send reverberating through my life. It was now nearly midnight and I peered out at the dark, dirty streets. Rome was empty. The sky was black and starless. I was only dimly aware of the policeman's hand cradling my own.

At the prison we were met by a frail, pleasant man in a grey suit and a grey, gentle face. He was the head warden. He looked me up and down, shook his head and somehow seemed upset that I was there. A woman entered the office, a round, stocky peasant who crooked her finger in my direction and motioned for me to follow her. We went to another room and once more I had to remove my clothes. In their place, I was given a pale, colourless blue pinafore and told to put it on. I wasn't wearing any jewellery except for a serpent ring with moonstone eyes and a long, twisting tail. The stones had belonged to my mother and the ring was designed by my beloved friend Augusto Torlonia – though why I was wearing it I can't imagine. For me, moonstones and serpents are both unlucky. I slipped the ring off and dropped it into the open mouth of an envelope.

'Please, take it home with you, keep it,' I told the woman. 'I never want to see it again.'

She gave me a harsh, intimidating stare and didn't reply. She scrutinized my hair, my clothes, my suntan and then went back to sorting through the rest of my belongings. Mysteriously, my cases and hand luggage had found their way to that particular little room before I did. The woman picked up each thing, examined it and then, in large, careful letters, wrote down what it was on an official form. I stopped her when she came to the two LP records.

'They're not mine,' I said. 'Can they be sent to my friend?'

'No, they can't,' the woman replied.

I had been put in my place. It was one of those them and us situations and, if I had committed a crime, the quality of my possessions added to my guilt. That thought was not to come to me until later, days later. As I stood there quietly waiting, I still felt as if the whole thing was happening to someone else. A part of me was standing behind my shoulder and watching with absolute detachment.

Eventually the woman finished her task and I signed for my things.

'Come this way,' she said, and I followed her out of the room and into the corridor. There was a man outside the door and, with him in the lead, me in the centre and the woman bringing up the rear, we moved off in single file down the corridor which appeared to narrow and lower as we went along. Bare bulbs covered in mesh were widely spaced along the walls, and between each island of gloomy yellow light were expanses of murky darkness.

We turned a corner, we kept walking and, as we did so, I could hear the sound of my heart beating in rhythm to the click, click, click of my heels, a sound that echoed like a funeral drum and rolled off into the distance. The passageway seemed endless. I had lost all sense of time and could have been falling down a well. I felt as if everything, my past, my life, reality, all were slipping away behind me.

Finally, we came to a halt. I passed through a wide, heavy door and listened while it was closed, the key turned and the bolts slid back into place. The first thing to hit me was the overpowering smell of disinfectant. It made my eyes sting. They were dry, as dry as the stone floor of the corridor. Not a tear had reached them. I felt no sadness but an overwhelming sense of shock.

In the half light I now saw three women. They had been talking. They stopped for a moment, focused on me and then lost interest. In the brief lull in conversation, I heard the dripping of a tap. The cell contained four wooden bunks. I climbed into the empty one, stretched myself out and stared unblinking at the ceiling. The women were prostitutes and talked about their trade. 'I always use a glove,' one voice was saying. 'I couldn't without it,' said another – words that for me had no meaning. I lay there, as motionless as a corpse. I couldn't understand why I had been so foolish. Harry was flying in from Montreal to be with me. He had finally severed all links with his wife and we were going to have the time and the freedom to allow our relationship to grow. Why hadn't I broken my links with Mario Schifano? What was I doing bringing his parcels from England? And how did the police know I was carrying something? It was all much deeper and bigger than I imagined that first night in prison. Not that I gave it that much thought: in my reverie, my mind kept spinning back to Harry.

Very soon after I lay down I began to tremble. I had all the symptoms of a drug addict without being one. The woman in the bunk opposite pulled a blanket over me, the conversation slowly faded, and I listened to the loud, steady dripping of the tap. It was like the Chinese water torture. I started to feel like a criminal, not because of what I had done but over everything that I might have done. I still didn't feel frightened, though it was a surprisingly short time before I began to think that I had been forgotten. I would be left forever in that odorous cell room, my body numb, my reasoning disjointed, doomed to stare forever at all the faces that formed in the damp stains above my head.

When that long night came to an end, I became aware of a buzz of excitement around me. In Italy, newspapers are delivered in prison but, if there are any articles about one of the prisoners, they are cut out.

That morning, the newspaper was in tatters: no front page, a gaping hole on page three, an even bigger hole on page five.

Through the whispers over the prison telegraph, the prostitutes had discerned that I was the cause of all this weighty censorship and, where they had treated my arrival in the cell with bored lack of interest, they now regarded me with utter fascination. To warrant such coverage at the very least I must have killed my lover, my lover's wife, my own three children. An endless parade of different eyes peered at me through the peephole in the door, my three companions stared, and now, of course, they tried to engage me in conversation. I didn't respond. I was in a state of trauma and couldn't speak.

I had imagined that I would be forgotten; the shredded newspaper showed that the very opposite was the case. There was no political news. Everyone was on holiday. At that time each summer, people could be dying and there would be no doctors to help them. Nothing was happening in the city, and my arrest suddenly provided all the right ingredients for bold headlines and the worst sort of sensationalism. It was the most discreditable thing to happen to a Franchetti since the burning of my ancestor, though my offence was far less exotic: she had been accused of seducing a monk. But still it was news. I was the first person from my social background to be involved in such a scandal and the media were making the most of it.

After the diversion of the newspapers, some food appeared, though I didn't eat and I didn't move until someone came and took me out of the cell and led me back along the dingy corridor to the office, where the chief warden sat hunched over his desk making notes. He told me to take a seat and studied me for several seconds, as if he wasn't too sure what to say.

'I don't think it is wrong for me to say that you are a lady,' he finally said. He paused and became serious and donnish: 'But you know, a lady should only be mentioned three times in her life – when she is born, when she marries and when she dies.'

He spoke as if he had known me a long time and was suddenly disappointed. I couldn't quite make out the point of his words, although they have stuck in my mind from that day to this. The other things he said were all the usual things people say ... it was terrible that it should have happened ... I had broken the rules ... I had become involved in something bigger than I realized ... it was upsetting for my family ...

'Your sister has arranged to come and see you later today.'

I nodded. I murmured my thanks and was then returned to my cell. I climbed back into the bunk and again remained motionless until the afternoon, when I was taken to the visitors' room.

In some ways, that room, even more than the cell and the spooky corridor, was the most incredible place that I was to see during the whole experience: the dust, the dirty, stained walls and the vast, ugly metal grille that divided the small area in two halves. Lorian was waiting on one side with Lollo and, when I walked in, I glanced around me and felt as if I really had killed my lover and three children. It was like being on Death Row. I almost expected to see a priest lurking in the shadows.

Lorian looked completely overwrought, as if she was the prisoner and I was visiting her. All her maternal instincts reached out to embrace me and for once the gap between us was bridged. She said many things – Lorian's a great talker – but I was still in such mental turmoil it was impossible to focus on her words.

'And don't worry, Afdera,' I kept hearing. 'We'll get you out of here as soon as we can.'

'Thank you,' I kept mumbling.

Lollo had been nodding eagerly. He now leaned forward and, when he spoke, his words broke through the mist and rang out like a bell.

'Harry's been informed.'

'I don't want to see Harry,' I sighed. 'Please don't contact him.'

'But Afdera,' Lollo implored. Before he could continue, Lorian stopped him.

'We can worry about all that another day,' she stressed. 'Let's get Afdera out of here first.'

My sister and brother-in-law exchanged long, careful stares with each other and then both switched their attention back to me.

We all remained silent for a few seconds. I glanced at Lollo. He was bristling with indignation and fine good health and I couldn't help wondering if my arrest would have an adverse effect on his political ambitions. I then looked at my sister. For all our similarities, we had far more differences, in our values, our principles, our very philosophies. At that precise moment there was even a difference in our colouring. She was drawn and pale, like all the people I had seen inside the prison. In my daze, the one thing I had noticed was that everyone was white and pasty, while I, in complete contrast, was dark brown and really at my very best. It was acutely embarrassing.

The conversation started up again and we talked about normal things until the visit came to an end. I was marched back to my cell. The day faded and I spent another night studying pictures of Harry in the damp stains that patterned the ceiling. I had to face one more night in the cell, and then I would be moved to a large, empty dormitory in the prison infirmary.

That came about immediately after I was given a thorough medical examination. In fact, the doctor couldn't find a single, solitary thing wrong with me, not even bad nerves or high blood pressure, but my records showed that I had suffered from polio as a child and that had left me too delicate for the rigours of normal prison life. I had a slightly crooked foot – I had forgotten which one, though I did limp a little when it came to the long walk to my new place of confinement, a room filled with sunshine and a view over a grey stone garden. It was just as well that I was taken out of the cell. Once the prostitutes had learnt that I wasn't a mass murderer, their fascination changed back once more to an attitude of supreme indifference. If I had remained locked away with them for three months, I would have discovered rather more than I wanted to know about a great number of things.

During the conversation I'd had with Lorian and Lollo, it was really Lorian who did all the talking, while I just tried to mumble the occasional response. My throat had dried up and I continued to show all the symptoms of a drug addict suffering from withdrawal – something I knew about from the time I had spent working as a nurse's aide. When it came to the second medical, my voice had diminished to an indistinct whisper. The doctor was filling in a form.

'What are you allergic to?' he asked.

'Aeroplanes,' I muttered.

'What medicines do you take regularly?'

I thought before I answered. 'Senokot.'

'Are you addicted to anything?'

'Harry,' I immediately croaked.

'I'm sorry?'

'Ha... Harry.'

The doctor must have thought that I was using a diminutive for a rare drug and wrote something down in Latin. I think it was one of those forms where it didn't so much matter what was said as long as all the spaces were filled.

When he left the dormitory, I drifted back once more into the dense, peculiar fog that had consumed my brain. Time had stretched out of shape and I was unable to concentrate on anything – a book, the view from the window, Lorian when she came with her messages and plans. The governor would occasionally drop in and then, one afternoon, the lawyer appointed to defend me made his first appearance. He spoke of 'bugging' and 'tapes' and things which, at that moment, didn't make the slightest bit of sense. The lawyer was short and vaguely handsome. He seemed permanently on the edge of excitement and, though I didn't have anything to say during his visits, I found them exhausting.

I was happiest when I was left on my own. I remained on the hard iron bed and spent long hours watching the squares of light on the infirmary wall change shape with the rising and setting of the sun. I didn't sleep a great deal, although when I did my dreams were no different from my thoughts. I tried to analyse myself and my life, but inevitably, like the revolving of a wheel, I came back to Harry. I knew, somehow I knew that I would never see him again.

Such were my thoughts for four days and four nights. Then, after all sorts of clever manoeuvrings by Lorian and my lawyer, the pair of them turned up at the infirmary with some clean clothes, I changed out of the colourless prison apron, and was released – not on bail, drug offences were too serious for that, but into the custody of a private clinic owned by Professore Cannizzaro, an old family friend who had agreed to take me in spite of the obvious embarrassment it would cause. My retinue included a young female warden and four armed guards who were to work in six-hour shifts outside my door.

By the time this move came, I had spent exactly one week in jail; by then I had come out of the initial deep shock and had entered a more peaceful, relaxed phase. Now I reached out for every book in sight and read endlessly, the same as when I was a child in the library at home. The hours vanished with P. G. Wodehouse, Nancy Mitford, Kafka, and I became more at ease in their worlds than in the real world of the clinic. One window of my room faced east and, when I wasn't reading, I enjoyed the view, the watered greenery below in the garden, the hills outside Rome and, beyond, the tall mountains veiled in clouds that disappeared into the distance. They led east; my mind wandered in the same direction. In prison I had decided that I no longer wanted to live, but the idea was only fleeting and not true to my inner instincts.

Whatever happens, I never lose my optimism. I didn't want to die, but to begin anew. I wanted to follow the mountains to the Orient and completely disappear. The plan was comforting; it stayed with me through the weeks and months that lay ahead, and even through the years that followed my eventual release.

Apart from the lawyer, only my family was allowed to visit me. Lorian came every day. She talked and I listened, and it was at this time that I learned how she had first been informed of my arrest. The news came from Tirletti, the astute top man at the Grand Hotel. He knew what was going on because some agents from the British branch of Interpol had gone to the hotel and searched both the room I had reserved there and the luggage I had had sent there from Turkey. He dug a bit deeper, discovered why I had failed to show up, and immediately let Lorian know. Tirletti was such a clever and discreet man that he was later taken out of the hotel and placed in Gianni Agnelli's Fiat organization. It was Gianni Agnelli, incidentally, who was one of the first people to call my sister with advice about lawyers. Another early caller was Augusto Torlonia, who was there, as always, promising to do whatever he could on my behalf.

I had always greatly valued my friends, and they were with me in my hour of need. Many letters and phone calls came from the United States and from all over Europe and, as Lorian gradually became the centre of attention, she started to enjoy every second of it. Several people offered to be character witnesses, including the financier Craig Mitchell, a fiery New York Irishman and one of my closest friends. During one of the periods when Harry and I had broken off our romance it was to Craig that I ran, and from then until this day we have remained close. Craig is a man with red hair and the temper of a giant; he was so fond of me that I was afraid that if he ever did manage to find his way to the Palazzo della Giustizia, he would lose his temper with the judge and I would end up with a life sentence.

Lorian went carefully through all the letters that were sent by my friends, though I actually read very few of them. I remember Nana, my aunt, writing to say how I had always been the black sheep of the family but that whatever happened she would continue to be there when I needed her. Marina Cicogna wrote about the memories we shared from childhood and related it all to the present, particularly my present set of circumstances. Annibale Scotti was as funny as ever: 'You're getting what you deserve, but we're still friends.'

He's still the same to this day, of course. He called me in London just recently. 'Afdera, guess what, darling?' he said. 'I've found a little island in the Caribbean called Scotti. Well, I just had to buy it.'

I didn't hear from Fonda – not that I expected to. He had a new life and a new wife; I was part of the past. Surprisingly, I thought less about my ex-husband than about his daughter. Jane is a woman with guts and it seemed to me that now, more than ever before, we could have found endless points of mutual understanding. Jane, with her great sense of compassion, is a woman who loves to fight for lost causes, and at that time I would have liked to have had her on my side fighting for me.

The best part of my routine in the clinic was the daily call by Professore Cannizzaro. There was nothing medically wrong with me, but as he checked on all of his patients he saw no reason to miss out on me, even if I was there under unusual circumstances. He was tall, handsome and every woman in Rome was in love with him, and it was a delight to listen to his nice, softly-spoken voice, even if now I can't remember what it was we talked about.

The hours went quickly with my books and my view over the eastern mountains, and the only part of the day that bored me were the visits of my lawyer. He came punctually at four, even when there were no new developments. I had nothing to say to him and when he could find nothing to say to me, he just sat and looked at me. My case was still receiving plenty of news coverage and the lawyer seemed to enjoy all the publicity that was spilling over on him.

It was through the lawyer that I now found out how the police had known that I was carrying marijuana. Mario Schifano was at the centre of a little circle of drug users and his telephone had been bugged. My lawyer had copies of the tapes. Since Mario also was a man who had plenty of ladies around him, some of the tapes were richly erotic and clearly made my lawyer rather excited.

In many ways, the predicament I had got myself into was inevitable when I got involved with Mario Schifano. His world and mine were at different parts of the galaxy and, though it was thrilling to enter his world, I knew that somehow, at some time, something would have to be sacrificed. I first met Mario when I was working with Ugo Mulas. I liked his studio, the loud music, the people who sat around the large wooden table discussing their wild theories. Those people were living for the day, without a past or future, commitment or security. It was all so fast and dramatic, it was joyous and suicidal, so creative and yet destructive. It was a magnet for my misty Gothic heritage, the hidden me that was rarely revealed. Harry was constantly in my heart but when, in that period, he went back to the safety of his old, familiar life, I went to Mario.

His studio was a rambling collection of rooms bare of furniture and stacked high with enormous canvases. He was the *enfant prodige* of all the Italian intellectuals. Men like Alberto Moravia, Renato Guttuso, Goffredo Parise (the author of *Il Prete Bello*), my cousin Giorgio Franchetti and many others mourned Schifano's arrest and contributed the money to pay for his lawyer. Mario introduced me to the music of the Rolling Stones; he spoke of Bob Dylan as if he was in love with him. Mario was something unique, talented, shadowy and, for me, the spring after a long, hard winter. It could never last, I didn't want it to last, but naturally, in accord with my character, when we parted we remained friends. That was why I found myself at the Ritz with one of his associates and the pathetic package containing three marijuana cigarettes.

During the years between my dismissal from *Vogue* and my arrest, Harry and I had kept each other in sight. We never let go, but we never held tight either. I had other romances with some very special men, but always, when it came to it, even if those men were kinder, nicer, better, stronger men than Harry, he was the one I loved. Even I wasn't completely sure why. He made me laugh. We could talk to each other. We enjoyed being together. He had the saddest face and the most wonderful smile. He was complicated, in many ways weak, especially when it came to making major decisions, but with that peculiar strength that such people have. He tended to get his own way, not by being forceful and demanding but by sitting back, saying nothing, and then doing exactly what he had planned to do. I loved him in spite of it. He loved my independence of will and spirit. Those things combined to grow into an umbilical cord that tied us together, even when we were apart. With the Little Man I had a closeness I didn't feel with anyone else, a closeness that became physical as well as cerebral. I rented out my apartment on Park Avenue and moved to Paris, where I lived for more than a year. It just seemed like a good idea at the time, though, on reflection, it may have been because Paris is only five minutes from London.

During that period, Harry went off with another woman, a lady with three children. All my friends said it was a tragedy and tried to comfort me. But I wasn't heartbroken at all. I knew Harry better than they did and I knew that this diversion was part of his long-term, even subconscious plan to find his way back to me.

It went on like this through months that crumbled away into years. Then, finally, he moved out of the family home, took an apartment in a building he had constructed in Montreal, and prepared the ground for the beginning of our life together.

It was then that I was arrested for carrying drugs.

With this, the most awful of ironies, to keep me company, the days in the clinic clicked by with a routine so regular and steady I didn't even notice them passing. I had my books, my vague visions of China and the Far East; I was almost contented. The woman who had to remain with me in the dining-table-sized room was forever trying to draw me into conversation, though we had nothing in common and really nothing to say to each other. The four men who guarded the door shared a gun that they came to see as being both unnecessary and too weighty to lug about. One of them eventually decided to leave it in a drawer in my bedside locker, and there it stayed – a fact that appealed to Lorian's sense of humour.

My sister continued to be supportive, although it was during my stay at the clinic that I came to realize that the division between us was something she maintained solely so that she didn't have to account too closely for my inheritance. When I got married, I gave her and Lollo power of attorney over my allowance and, when Mama died, I extended this to the money left to me in the estate. That money had been invested, and somehow the investment had gone wrong. I didn't exactly know why. It was something we didn't discuss, although the presence of the unresolved question was permanently there, like a little sore we were afraid to touch in case we broke the scab and made it worse.

Lorian and Lollo, when he came, would often talk about Harry, but I refused to be drawn out. I was certain that he would want nothing to do with me, and, for his sake, I wanted no more to do with him. I tried to push him out of my mind. I tried so hard that when, one evening, Professore Cannizzaro came for his daily visit and I saw a little figure in white like a shadow behind him, I couldn't believe my eyes.

I was only allowed visits by my lawyer and members of my family. But strings had been pulled. The head of the clinic was a man with great humanity and understanding. He stood motionless for a couple of seconds and then faded from the room. The female warden wasn't there. The guard closed the door and I heard his footsteps as he disappeared along the passage. I was alone with the Little Man.

It was so strange to see him – and even stranger to see him dressed in the long white coat of a doctor. The silence stretched out, as vast as the universe. We looked at each other as if it was yesterday, or a tomorrow deep in the distant future. A tiny fragment of a smile crept on to his lips and then he said something – something very English, funny, but in that dry English way. I didn't laugh. I didn't smile. I struggled to find my voice.

'I really don't want to see you. I can't see you,' I said. 'I can only harm you ... your career, your life.'

He just stood there smiling.

'Please don't make it more hurtful,' I pleaded. 'Leave me, leave me now.'

'Certainly not,' he replied.

'It must be such a shock for everyone,' I went on. 'I love you ... and it's because I love you that I never want to see you again.'

There was another long silence. Harry's smile had slipped away and now I looked into his dark eyes and saw a tenderness in them that I had never seen before.

'It's because I love you that we will be together ... and stay together,' he then said.

We embraced, the embrace became an act of love. Once more our words drifted away; and when it was time for him to leave and I watched the door closing behind him, I immediately began to wonder if the whole thing had been a dream.

It wasn't a dream. Harry came disguised as a doctor many times. He visited Lorian and Lollo and, when my sister and I were alone after that visit, she told me that he talked constantly about the future we were going to share. I was pleased, though never fully convinced. Those seeds of doom had been growing from the very day we met and danced together at Kitty Miller's ball in London. I knew deep down that, whatever castles we built, something would come along and destroy them. I'm not a pessimist; it was an intuition.

The weeks became months and, when three had passed, it was time for my trial. I wore a military-style dress and coat, a faint tan had clung to my skin, my eyes were far away and my expression seemed somewhat detached. I had spent very little time in front of the mirror while I was in the clinic and, when I studied myself that morning, it didn't look like me at all. My armed guards collected their gun, we ambled out into the autumn sunshine, and I was taken in a convoy of police cars to the main court at the Palazzo della Giustizia. It was an enormous chamber, with the press boxes overflowing and the public gallery almost empty. My friends hadn't forgotten me: they stayed away in silent protest and support.

I stood in a tall wooden dock, I glanced around – and there was Mario Schifano, incredibly, in chains.

'*Embe, hai portato almeno i dischi?*'

He was quite an amazing man. The first thing he asked me was for the two records that had come from England. I told him they were still in Rebibbia and we said no more.

The judge appeared and the trial began.

My lawyer rose, sweaty and hysterical beneath his white wig, and as soon as he spoke he got himself tied up in knots. I saw the years of my prison sentence stretching into eternity, but then Avvocato Gatto, the man chosen by the intellectuals to represent Mario, began to speak on my behalf, and the judge slowly softened. He explained that I had been arrested before passing through passport control and was therefore technically still outside the frontier of Italy. The judge nodded gravely. I was fined and, more humiliatingly, I was placed on probation for three years.

Schifano was also released. He had been in the awful Regina jail for more than three months and that should have been punishment enough – though obviously not. He was back in prison six months later on another drugs offence and, since then, has been in and out of confinement several times. It is while he is in prison that he becomes inspired; the exhibitions he has upon release are more highly praised each time.

The trial was a quiet, straightforward affair until its dying moments. Then, the main doors crashed open at the back of the court room and a wild man entered, throwing punches at everyone within his reach.

I stared in disbelief: it was my brother Nanuck.

157

'Why can't you leave us in peace?' he was shouting. 'Who are these dreadful people who want photographs and gossip?'

'Put him out! Put him out!' The judge had come to his feet, he was pounding his gavel and yelling at the court officials.

'It's Barone Franchetti,' I heard a voice whisper.

'These people are scum,' Nanuck yelled, and he struck out with both fists until a small army of men managed to restrain him. Nanuck was then taken to the cells, where he remained until the court adjourned.

I didn't go to see him. As soon as the trial was over, my lawyer drove me to the airport and I flew straight to Montreal.

11 . *Kite on the Wing*

Montreal, and the world was again my oyster: new friends, a new beginning and, finally, I was with the man of my life. It should have been wonderful, but I was feeling insecure. The clinic had been like a womb and I wasn't ready to cope with the sudden strains of reality. I was so glad to be with the Little Man, yet at the same time I resented the fact that it had taken my arrest for him to reach a decision about us. Was it compassion or was it love?

Harry's divorce was going through slowly, but without too many dramas. I had decided to cut my ties with New York and sold my apartment, although my friends were still all there, as loyal as always, which made me wonder if I was doing the right thing. Those friends thought it was so romantic that, after so long and after such an ordeal, I was finally with the man I loved, although they weren't aware of my new feeling of insecurity.

When the flat had gone, my Italian furniture, and a warehouse of belongings I had managed to accumulate, were shipped back across the Atlantic, without Fidalma and Giuseppe – unless, of course, by this time Giuseppe was the owner of the shipping line.

My things went to Denbies, the house where Harry had lived all his life and which he loved so very much. Alide and Adriana, Harry's servants, were waiting there when we returned from Canada to live in England, which made me feel most at home. This is where we spent our weekends, although I also took a small *pied à terre* in Eaton Square. Having my own roof over my head was what I needed and, little by little, I regained my old feeling of independence. In Montreal I had tried in my own way to be a geisha, but I was not good at it. True, once in a while I did get up and cook the Little Man his breakfast before he went to the office, though unfortunately there were also times when the little briefcase was thrown at the Little Man. Thank God, it was usually empty except for a few bills, mostly from my telephone calls, and the same old copy of *Playboy* that had been there for months.

The weekends at Denbies were always eventful. People kept flocking in – and, here and there, the briefcase was still flying. My Italian friends would come, people like the Lloyd's underwriter Marino de la Garda, whom I had known since childhood, and his wife Maria Grazia, whom Harry, thank God, liked immediately. D-D-David Metcalfe came every week with a different woman, which I found most unsettling. I finally met Harry's sister, Rosalind Shand, a forceful lady and very different from her brother. She was marvellous, ruthless, outspoken; she reminded me of my own family. It was she who advised me to have a baby – which would serve to bring Harry and me closer together – or alternatively to go away, and wait for Harry to sort out his own thoughts on our future. They were both probably good suggestions, but just at that time I didn't have the courage to cope with either of them.

Harry and I spent the weekends with friends, and lots of holidays – really too many, for instead of bringing us together these had the opposite effect. We both had mysterious, tangled pasts; we were two negatives, but instead of this making a positive, everything became doubly negative. It was a vicious circle: although we were never happy apart, we stopped being happy together. By the time Harry's divorce was finalized, Harry and I had already been through more than most married couples – so much more that to have then got married would have brought us less joy than sorrow. I have never stopped loving him in my own way; I don't know if he loved me or not, but, little by little, small things happened that finally made us decide we had to break up. It had been ten years from the first time we had met, and we would always remain friends.

In the days that followed, I had plenty of time for reflection. I realized how many opportunities I had squandered or taken for granted over the years – my marriage to Fonda, for instance. I felt a tremendous sense of failure at not having been able to make the relationship work with Harry, the only man I every really cared for. I was full of contradictory thoughts and emotions: I felt no self-pity and recognized that I had to change; I felt like a volcano about to explode, yet I was trapped in a kind of limbo. I knew I ought to take charge of my life and find a useful job, and yet, instead, all I really wanted to do was run away.

I soon settled in a charming little house in Caroline Terrace, the house that I have liked most of all, and Adriana and Alide would appear periodically with different things that I had been keeping in boxes at Harry's house in the country. One of these things was a painting of a camel by Tiepolo that had belonged to Mama and had hung in her bedroom throughout the years of my childhood. I was by no means hard up at this time, but I needed some ready cash and so I decided to sell the painting at Sotheby's.

I went along to the auction with some women friends. We were planning to put our hands up to make the bidding go higher, but we arrived too late and, while we were still catching our breath, the hammer fell and the Tiepolo had gone. We weren't interested in the other items, so off we all went to have a pizza. We were all dying to know who had bought the painting, but it had all happened so quickly none of us saw a thing.

That evening I was going out to dinner with some friends and one of them, Dominic Elliott, a clever property developer from Scotland, had come to pick me up. He was sitting in the drawing-room and I was busy getting ready when there was a ring at the door. There on the doorstep was a delivery man with a disgusting parcel wrapped in dirty newspaper. He thrust it into my arms and fled. I immediately thought it was a bomb and screamed. Dommie rushed to the rescue and, using just the tips of his fingers, slowly peeled back the newspaper to reveal – my little camel. The next day I found out that it was the Little Man who had bought the painting, so that it could be mine again. Only Harry could have done such a thing.

I put my painting back on the wall, I cashed the cheque from the auctioneers and set off for New York. The city was very social and filled with nostalgic memories, but I was still in the mood for quiet and therefore set off once again, this time for Sibilla O'Donnell's house in Nassau. For me, it was always such a joy to go there. The house is in the middle of the town, surrounded by native homes, behind a long stone wall that is always covered in bright bougainvillaea. Once inside that wall, you are surrounded by the tranquillity of a completely different world. Everything is made of wood. Pastel-coloured flowers are every-where and there is a swimming pool that has been brought all the way from Naples.

I arrived on Thursday, spent all day in the sun, and by Friday morning I was peeling and as red as a lobster. It was actually Good Friday, and, by complete coincidence, the thirteenth of the month. That evening there was a dinner party.

'I've put you next to somebody you don't know,' Sibilla said. 'He's a very controversial Irishman, and the only white magistrate here, though his work is more like that of a judge.'

So I sat next to the controversial magistrate, though I must admit that he was paying far more attention to the gorgeous blonde on his other side. He was also called away from the table every few minutes, which I found rather intriguing. When he did manage to stay seated long enough for me to be able to say something, I started to ask him to pass me things – the salt, the pepper, the bread. From there we fell into conversation and he told me that the following day a man was to be hanged. As Assistant Chief Justice, he was acting as judge and coroner, and various people were still trying to stop the execution. It was the first hanging on the island for twelve years, so naturally everyone was interested, even a bit frightened.

'So, I'm going to do my duty tomorrow and then I'm going to get completely sloshed.'

The magistrate's name was John Bailey and I thought he was witty and marvellous. He was refreshingly different from all the people I had left behind in England.

'I shan't see you tomorrow because I shall be busy all day,' he said. 'We shall meet again at church on Sunday and then you're having lunch with me.'

He took it for granted that I would be at church – but, as it turned out, I didn't make it. I was delighted to find the house empty and stayed at home, on my own, sunbathing. John appeared after the service.

'What are you doing here?' he demanded. 'Come on, it's almost time for lunch.'

I shrugged, obeyed his instructions and followed him to his house, a simple little place far out on the point, surrounded by beaches and with long views over a soft, motionless sea. The house turned out to be full of people, mainly beautiful women, and I didn't feel at all at ease. John recognized this; he even had the same feeling himself. The hanging had been traumatic, of course, but he was a man who had just gone through an emotional crisis and recognized the same after-effects in me. We concluded that falling in love was a dreadful disease.

'Never again,' I said.

'Never again,' he agreed.

We wandered away from the rest of the people, climbed into a small motor boat and slowly carved a path across the transparent aquamarine sea. Schools of tiny fish followed our progress, darting in and out of the coral, parting and regrouping as if bound by a single thread and a single consciousness. We drifted to a halt. The island was small and deserted, quiet but for the humming birds that whispered through the trees. John, with the *forza della natura* in his Irish blood, immediately drew me into an embrace that, between the peeling sunburn and the crusty surface of the rocks, turned out to be both painful and very, very pleasant.

After staying a further week in the Bahamas, I returned to London. John came to meet me in August – on the thirteenth. We flew to Cork and then set out to see the beautiful Irish countryside he so loved. I don't think we missed a single pub all the way from Cork to Tralee. John was a working-class man who was very ambitious and on the way up. After his ten years in the Bahamas he had become more sophisticated, but he had never lost his rough, genuine side and was still very much at home with the local people, though they now looked at him through different eyes. He showed me the house where he had been born and where his mother, brother and sister still lived. It was the very house where the song 'The Rose of Tralee' was written.

John Bailey wasn't a romantic, but one evening he took me to the village cemetery and showed me the tomb where all his family were and the rest would be buried.

'If you want, one day you could be buried there,' he said.

I thought it was a sweet and unusual way to show one's feelings.

The timing of my meeting with John Bailey was perfect. He was the right person to help me get over what had been a painful and rather destructive period in my life.

John left the Bahamas to take a post as a district judge in Hong Kong. It was a step up the ladder for him and, though he had shown some reluctance to take the job, I did everything I could to persuade him. During the long, quiet days I had spent dreaming in the clinic, it was to China that I had wanted to run away and disappear forever. With John going there, my fantasy now seemed like some magic sign, and my going too was the most natural thing in the world.

I joined him a month after his arrival, flying out of London on the long journey and, strangely, realizing, for the first time, that I had little fear. The plane flew around the island three or four times and I looked down and could see all the little fishing junks returning from the deeps. I could see Repulse Bay, the cemetery on the hill with a procession of white-clad people and the hills full of skyscrapers all pressed so tight one against the other.

Finally I saw the skinny finger of the runway poking out into the sea. The engines changed tone. I held my breath and we came into land.

John was there, running and breathless as always.

'I hate this place,' he said straight away. He paused and then added: 'I'm glad you're here.'

Unlike John, I didn't hate the place. Far from it. I felt an instant chemistry from the moment I arrived, a feeling that wasn't to change throughout the four or five years during which I spent long periods there with John.

The luggage was loaded into a taxi and we set off on the long journey from the airport to the Lee Gardens Hotel, where we were to stay until John had found an adequate apartment. From the taxi window I looked out and had my first glimpse of the rich and colourful life, the streets teeming with people, everything appearing so disorganized until you looked closer and saw how clean and neat and ordered everything really was. Outside the shops there were strings of goods. The merchants were all busy and smiling. There was so much colour, so much vitality it seemed to awaken in me the same spirit of barter that had belonged to the ancient Franchetti traders who moved goods from North Africa to Venice and probably to and from China as well.

In the weeks that followed I found myself each day wandering alone while John was in court and feeling completely at home in the narrow, overfilled streets. There I took to browsing round the stalls for bargains with such eagerness it was clear that I was really just a nomad and, in my own way, an explorer, like Papa. In the same way that he felt at home among the natives of Africa, I felt at ease with the Orientals. Now, for the first time, I began to understand a little bit more about my father and the sort of man he was.

During those daily walks I purchased more and more items, and within a week the hotel room at Lee Gardens was so full of clutter we couldn't move. I found so many interesting things: little baskets, stone eggs on wooden stands, live birds in a cage shaped like a castle. Something else that particularly fascinated me was that, although millions of

Chinese for thousands of years have kept birds in bamboo cages, the cages all disappear. What did remain were the tiny, hand-made porcelain containers used for the food and water. These were sold in the junk shops all around Cat Street, some almost new and some many hundreds of years old. I started to collect them – a collection I continued when I eventually began my trips to Mainland China.

John, who was a bachelor with no sense of possessions, wasn't sure he liked all this clutter but, as a man with a good nose for a bargain, when he learnt that I was doing rather well with my purchases, he let me continue to fill every available space in the room.

Eventually John, with the luck of the Irish and a few intrigues, was able to find a bungalow which would normally have only been given to a father with five children and a high establishment job.

Once we settled in the bungalow, life became different. For the first time in my life I had to become domesticated, with no Fidalma and Giuseppe, Adriana and Alide, or Tirletti from the Grand Hotel, but with a very ambitious, and stingy, young man. He did finally concede me an amah, mostly because he realized that without one, life would have been exceedingly complicated. John could wander around the house naked, but in court he needed polished shoes and trousers that were creased in the right places – though even in court he never wore socks.

The amahs were a unique race. They all wore the same uniform – black trousers, slippers and black Chinese jackets – but by their earrings you knew what category they were. Coral was worn by the first grade, turquoise by the middle and pearls by those at the top. Our amah wore pearls. She chose us, rather than we choosing her. She liked us and so she stayed.

Every week, John gave me a hundred Hong Kong dollars to do all the household shopping. We were going out quite a lot with new friends, John's civil service colleagues and their Eurasian wives, who taught me to cook, and some of my friends would drop in from time to time from England and America. With all these people to meet, it was pleasant when we did occasionally have an evening at home. John always wondered why at those times he was served the same dish – cabbage, bacon and boiled potatoes – though it was he who had once said that those were his favourite foods. The main reason I kept serving it was that I could buy all the ingredients in the Chinese open market under the bridge for $5 and then invest the rest in Cat Street. In those days, you could buy five dozen quails' eggs for practically nothing, so I always served them for starters.

All the time I was in Hong Kong (on and off between 1971 and 1976), I was aware of Mainland China like a great sleeping giant reaching out to embrace us from across the narrow strip of water. I looked out from the window of our bungalow and it seemed to call me, a mute echo from my long-ago visions at the clinic in Rome. There was something inside me, the explorer, the adventurer, something that made me want to see the land of the ancient emperors and warlords before it changed pace and began to move in step with the rest of the world. It was still difficult to go there except on business or in organized groups, but through the efforts of Joachino Mathis, an Italian diplomat in Peking, I finally managed to get a visa and set off on the early morning train from Kowloon, with Peking, the Forbidden City, my ultimate destination.

It was February, quite cold and with a clear blue sky contrasting in picture-book colours with the fields and small forests that punctuate the journey through the New Territories towards China. The train itself was a bit like the Orient Express, with deep, fat armchairs, the arms and backs covered in crisp linen cloths, little table lamps that threw out an amber glow, and a polished wood surround that gleamed with the years of care and attention. Everything was neat, clean, looked-after – so very different from the chrome and vinyl that I had been used to on European trains.

That same neatness could be seen from the window. As I passed through symmetrically cut paddy fields I saw the women working, all with the same large, distinctive hats, with clothes that were immaculate and with an elegance that makes me aware how proud the people are to be a part of the revolution that is taking China out of medieval poverty into an era of equality that might one day be the envy of the world.

After three or four hours, the train chugged to a halt at the entrance of a tunnel and I had to get out, carry my own luggage and pass through the tunnel on foot. Somewhere in the darkness there was a hidden camera that took my photograph and then I was on file. When I eventually emerged into daylight, I entered a large room, where the officials busied themselves with my papers and no one was able to hear what anyone else was saying because of the scratchy radio that played at full volume featuring a continuous chorus of singing children.

Above the noise, the immigration man managed to ask me if I had come to China on business.

'No,' I replied. 'I just came.'

'Yes?' He had the same inscrutable smile they all have.

'I came to see and to touch and to smell.' I thought about it and then added: 'And to eat.'

He thought I was very peculiar, but he stamped my passport all the same. I now had to change some money. You are not allowed to take any foreign currency into the country and it is here, at the border, that you exchange the amount you are going to need during your stay, leaving anything you have remaining to be collected when you depart.

I climbed back on board the train and continued on to the city of Canton, where I spent the night in a very uncomfortable hotel room. The next day I went on a sight-seeing tour, which turned out to be boring, except for one small shop that sold the same bird-cage containers that I had started collecting in Hong Kong. Surprisingly, they were very expensive.

In the museum, as in the restaurant the night before and in all the public buildings, the deafening sound of children's voices came bursting from a million hidden radios with the scratchy resonance of a wind-up gramophone – and always, always the same song.

Later that day I made my way to the airport and took a plane to Peking. When we landed in Peking an official boarded the plane and bowed obsequiously to one of the passengers, an immaculately dressed Japanese and he, after bowing back, moved slowly through the exit door. As the only woman on board, I was ushered along behind him and, as I stood on the top of the aeroplane steps, I looked out and couldn't believe my own eyes. There were twenty-five thousand uniformed schoolchildren all singing at the top of their tiny voices. They were in an enormous semi-circle around the plane, like a carpet. Flags were waving, everyone was grinning and I thought, my God, what a welcome. It was some minutes before I found out that the welcoming ceremony was for the Japanese man, who had come to take up his post as the first ambassador from that country to Peking.

I went to bed early because I had to be up early to see one of the famous and unique sights of Peking – luckily, something I could see from my bedroom window. It was six in the morning. Tens of thousands of bicycles were stacked against every available tree and, all in time together like a monster with a million tentacles, the working people were doing their physical exercises. It went on for about ten minutes and then, as if a whisper had reached every pair of ears at the same time, everyone got back on the bicycles and raced off to work. The day had begun.

During my first few days I took all the ordinary tours. I actually found the Great Wall disappointing and, although I enjoyed seeing the animal statues that line the avenue to the Ming Tomb, the tomb itself was really nothing very special. As so often happens, I was far more interested in watching the people, and was fascinated by the small children with their little round yellow faces and their little round blue bottoms that appear from trousers cut in a way that I have never seen anywhere else in the world. Strange, but a very good idea.

China was less a country to observe than to experience through the senses. Everything was in the process of change and yet much that was valuable from the nation's ancient traditions had also survived, the two blending together in unique harmony. I visited other cities and made further journeys to China, although I never altered my initial impressions: the neatness and cleanliness of the towns and villages, everywhere so many people, not with the common, robotic mind that is sometimes portrayed, but with a keen sense of individuality. There is in them a detachment, a certain nobility, a great curiosity; all combined. It made me feel sure that the prophecy of Nostradamus would one day come to pass. They would unite and rule the world.

Virtually every year for as long as I can remember, whether Hong Kong has been a feature or not, I have spent the summers in Italy, first sailing with friends and then doing the rounds of family visits. Whatever I say, or may have said, all families have their feuds, but in the final analysis, it is the people who belong to you who matter most. I love them all dearly.

It was 1982, the middle of August, and I had arrived in Venice. I was passing through the crowds on the Piazza San Marco – the most elegant drawing room in the world – when I saw a journalist I knew from London and stopped to have a drink in the Caffè Florian. The orchestra was playing. The pigeons moved in shifting grey clouds. San Marco loomed above us, a great monument to something timeless, without being eternal, perhaps a great truth we have lost, or even an enormous lie. Like all ancient buildings, it contained the echoes of all the heartbeats and memories of the multitudes that had entered its high arched doors, though to me, muted and cold. I went there often as a child, but never since. It made me feel uncomfortable, and instead of being uplifted by the murals that glowed in the candlelight, I would drop my head and study the intricate mosaics that patterned the floor.

My companion was the right sort of person to be with. Venice always found me in a strange mood and he knew how to be present, connected, yet silent. He had a haunted look, a face that was young, but sculptured by the experience of an old soul. His eyes were green or brown, depending on the light, with a liveliness that reminded me of Ugo Mulas.

We watched the people. Tourists carrying cameras and wearing gaudy clothes. A group of nuns in grey and black, a bit like the pigeons, nodding and chirping, bent over with weighty knowledge. An elderly man pulled out a violin and joined in with the café musicians. As his bow touched the strings a smile fixed itself to his lined brown face. Endless tiny thoughts passed through my mind like carnival floats, drawn from each worn stone, each fluted pillar, the archways and passageways. There had been a sudden cloudburst and now the gilded domes of the church sparkled in the sunshine. I had provoked my memories by sitting at the table where Mama had sat on summer afternoons. I would spend the day at the Lido with Marina Cicogna, Adriana Ivancich, Andriana Marcello – depending on what friend was in vogue. Like all young girls, we went through phases of being the best of friends and the worst of enemies. Mama would be at her table, Anna Maria Cicogna at the next and Vendramina Marcello next to her; those two grand old ladies are still today at the centre of Venetian social life. I would be sunburned, covered with salt and, depending on the strictness of the governess, carrying my shoes instead of wearing them. How I managed to wander all those years through the dirty summer streets without catching a disease, I'll never know.

These were the gentle years before tourism had become such a plague and the piazza really was a drawing room, its corners filled with writers and artists, the established, as well as the young, the actors and film-makers who were on the way up. They must have seen the young girl with no shoes on her feet and I wonder if they recognized her when she appeared at the festivals and parties a decade later. I was still taking my shoes off even then.

My companion at Florian's bought a newspaper from a passing vendor and his pale face became even more drawn and pale. He gently touched my arm and pushed the newspaper across the table. Fonda's face stared out from the front page. Below was the headline: HENRY FONDA È MORTO.

It took my breath away just for a moment. Then I smiled.

'He had a good life,' I said.

'Yes, I suppose he did,' came the reply.

I wasn't so surprised. I had seen Hank just a short time before on television, after he received the long-deserved Oscar for his performance in *On Golden Pond*. Jane Fonda was at the ceremony to collect the award for her father and, after her speech, the camera went inside his home in California. Fonda was tired and old, but with that peaceful look that comes to people when they realize that they have run the course to the best of their ability and are nearing the finish line. He was wearing an oversized navy-blue sweater and had a thick white beard that made me think immediately of Moses. His eyes were peering about him as if he was looking for something, or someone.

It was Jane's energy that had put Hank together with Katharine Hepburn to play the film's aging married couple, with herself as the prodigal daughter – a part that belonged to real life even more than it belonged to the story. After all her many changes, Jane had turned full circle and was back to being what she always was: her father's daughter. The fact that she had spoken out so vehemently against the war in Vietnam and thus, to American eyes, against America, only to go on and make a fortune as the body-beautiful queen of the exercise mat, isn't so much hypocritical as it is indicative of a person able to explore the very extremes of her potential. Henry Fonda, aged seventy-eight, was a man who had done exactly the same thing.

I saw the film *On Golden Pond* at a small theatre on Kings Road one afternoon with a lonely friend who had just become a widower. The cinema was almost empty, which made the sound of my sporadic laughter boom out through the silence like cannon shots. Some people obviously must have thought the storyline was sad, but to me it wasn't. It was full of humorous little ironies, some private to Hank and Jane and having absolutely nothing to do with the script. They were playing out scenes from their own turbulent biography, drawing on memories, rather than experience, to give performances worth a crate full of Oscars.

Some of the incidents were so amusing, I explained the relevance to my companion and he laughed even louder than I did.

When the lights came on for the intermission a man turned round and glared at us with a furious expression.

'Why are you laughing, it's not funny,' he said angrily.

'Of course it is,' my friend replied. 'It's very funny.'

'It's just the way he is in life,' I confided.

'Well I think you're wrong,' the man continued. 'I don't think it's funny at all.'

'She should know. She was married to him,' my friend then said.

'Yes, and I was married to Greta Garbo,' the angry man sneered. He got up and moved to the other side of the theatre.

The lights went down and when I watched the second half of the film I still found it amusing. Then I went home on my own, thought about the past and felt just a little sad.

There were two other meetings with Fonda that came back to my mind while I sat there quietly in that great square in Venice. The first was about six months after we were divorced. I had had a minor operation in New York and Hank took me to Martha's Vineyard, where he had rented a beach house, to recuperate. It was like a honeymoon. We strolled slowly arm in arm along the sand like lovers. It was the end of the season and the sea was whipped into waves by the autumn wind; gold and yellow leaves blew around our feet. A new love had entered my heart, but I was happy that Henry Fonda was still at my side.

That evening we went to the house owned by Lillian Hellman, but it was locked up for the winter and no one was there. I was glad. We went home, built a big log fire and pretended that it really was a honeymoon!

After that long weekend, we met several more times during the following twelve months. Then Hank met Shirlee, his last wife, and our secret little complicity drew to a close.

The last time we saw each other was a complete and magical coincidence. He was appearing in a two-hour, one-man stage play about the turn-of-the-century lawyer Clarence Darrow, who used to take only impossible cases that he believed in – and then, by some miracle, take them to court and win a just verdict. It was perfect for Fonda. It had been a great success on Broadway and he had brought the show to the West End – in spite of being over seventy and having a pacemaker and all sorts of other things. He loved to work. The schedule was arduous and the reviews, as ever, were wonderful. I had never closed the door on our friendship, and naturally I was dying to see him. Shirlee, however, was very protective. I was still a small ghost in the background and so, instead of calling directly, I contacted Margaret Littman, a mutual friend from my Hollywood days, a woman from the deep South who had coached Elizabeth Taylor, among many others, in the art of the Southern accent. She was a good friend of Truman Capote and they sounded identical. I asked her if she thought it would be all right if I asked the Fondas to dinner.

The line went dead.

'Better no,' Margaret Littman then answered. 'To Shirlee, you know, you're still Rebecca ...'

'But that's idiotic after so many years,' I broke in (like a sponge I had picked up the drawl). 'So much water has gone under the bridge.'

'I know, I know. She's so protective ...'

That was the very word in my mind. It seemed typical of American women, or rather some American women, and so I let it drop.

At this time, I was living in a charming house in Wilton Crescent, one of the nicest roads in Belgravia and the whole of London. I had learned how to cook and, having done all the shopping for John Bailey, I knew how to choose the meat and vegetables when someone was coming for a meal. One day when a dinner party was planned for the evening, I set off with my shopping bags to Elizabeth Street. I went first to the butcher's and then, as I was about to enter the greengrocer's, I saw a figure approaching from the distance who looked strangely familiar. It was a bright afternoon, the sun was in my eyes and I couldn't quite focus.

Then I heard the voice.

'Afdera.'

I shook my head in disbelief. It was Hank. Who else? He was wearing an old denim shirt that I remembered from twenty years before and under his arm he carried a large sketch pad with bulldog clips clamped along the side. His face was deeply lined and worn, a bit like a fisherman, his eyes were alert and as boyish as ever and his grey hair was dyed reddish brown for his role on stage. We embraced very tightly.

'Afdera, Afdera,' he kept saying.

'How wonderful, how wonderful,' I kept saying.

'You look marvellous ...'

'You look marvellous . . .'

The street was almost deserted, but anyone who did happen to pass by couldn't help but stop and stare in amazement.

'Where are you going?' he then asked.

'To the fruit shop.'

'So am I,' he laughed. 'I've got to buy some mushrooms.'

'To eat?'

'No, to paint,' he answered.

We both laughed and went inside.

His eyes lit up: 'Look at that fresh basil,' he said.

'How long are you staying?'

'Ah, there's the mushrooms.'

'Can you come to dinner?'

'You really do look marvellous, Afdera. You haven't changed a bit, you know . . .'

It went on for another ten minutes as if we were both characters in a Beckett play, neither of us responding to a single thing the other was saying but going off on our own wild tangents. The assistants were watching, rooted to the spot, and somewhere in the chaos I heard someone whisper: 'That's Henry Fonda . . .'

Hank pointed at some nice shiny eggplants.

'Hey, you remember when we had stuffed eggplants that night? They were delicious,' he said. 'Who was it that was coming . . .'

'I can't think . . .'

'Of course, it was Merle. She loved them.'

'Listen, how long are you staying in London?'

He was studying the mushrooms and now, when he turned back to look at me, his eyes clouded over and I realized that even if Hank wanted to bend his long legs under my table and join my friends at dinner, it was something that was not to be. We continued to talk, little things like buoys that bobbed in the great ocean of the past. He bought his mushrooms. I bought my fruit. Outside on the pavement we held hands and then we embraced again, our cheeks touching and carrying us back to La Cabala in Rome. The dim lights reflected from the mirrored ball that revolved above us and the band began to play 'On the Sunny Side of the Street'. In that short moment we were dancing, the tall man in his high-necked military uniform and the young woman who would leave the odd safety of her family to become his bride. We loved each other as we had always loved each other, though in a way that few would understand. Fonda was the father I never had and, as one would with a father, I wanted to keep him forever in my life. We didn't discuss it, but both of us were aware of this special and unusual feeling.

We parted and I watched him go, frail and bent over, his bag of mushrooms in his hand and his sketch pad under his arm. I wondered then, as I had often wondered before, what might have happened in my life had my father lived and met Henry Fonda. I'm sure they would have liked each other and immediately become friends. They were similar in many ways, ruthless yet gentle men; men of many sides with that rare blend of power and charisma that set them off on enormous challenges and kept them going until they reached their goals.

As Fonda disappeared around the corner, I remembered being the little girl of three, the light piercing the stained-glass windows in the drawing room of that strange, pre-Raphaelite villa at Sestri Levante. Simba, Lorian and Nanuck had marched away in their uniforms and a calm had settled upon the room. Papa was in an armchair, the great lion with the smallest of his cubs. He looked at me for a long time and then he glanced at Mama and said something that made her smile. I've no idea what it was he said, but I know it made me feel warm and happy inside.

The clouds above Venice had passed and the piazza was lit by that fresh clean light that follows the rain. I had taken my shoes off and put them on the chair opposite. My friend called for the bill. I folded the newspaper, and as I did so, I felt something plop on to my shirt. A pigeon was climbing high above and on my shoulder was a brown volcano in a yellow lake – the pigeon's promise of luck and good fortune.

12 . The Beginning

The telephone was ringing just as I was about to go out. I had half a mind not to go back, but, in the end, I did. It was a friend inviting me to spend the evening at the theatre the following week.

'I don't know, I hate making plans,' I said.

'There will be someone there you don't know, I'm sure you'll be pleased to meet him.'

'Yes, maybe.'

'And afterwards we can go out to dinner at . . .'

My friend mentioned the name of the restaurant and the name of the play which was all the rage, and in the end, I agreed to go.

Thus it goes on. Always the same and always different, cycles constantly revolving. Naturally, I return often to Venice, like a bird on migration or a criminal to the scene of the crime; and it was on one of those trips that I saw Lorian.

I was having lunch at Harry's Bar with a crowd of Nanuck's children, Bianca, Alberto, Letizia and Allegra. We were drinking masses of *bellini*s, talking about this and that and, ultimately, of my sister. I had arrived in town that day and she was leaving the next. There was little chance that we would meet, and perhaps that was for the better. After lunch, while Venice was empty, I went to Carol's, the hairdresser's where I have been going since I was a young woman. My hair was done and I emerged at three in the afternoon. You could have fallen over in the street and died and no one would have noticed, it was so deserted. I set out on the long Calle Larga San Marco towards the Bridge of San Moisè and, as I was walking, I saw a single figure cross the bridge and walk towards me. It was Lorian.

She was wearing dark glasses. So was I. I could feel, even from the distance, her two eyes looking me up and down. I did the same. It was like the final scene from *High Noon*; it was as if we were both waiting for the other to go for her gun. Slowly, we drew nearer and nearer. We met.

'My God,' I said in English.

'Oh, God,' Lorian said.

We passed and I listened as her footsteps disappeared behind me.

The previous year my sister had been touched by the extreme pain of losing a son, an accident that had distressed the whole family and a tragedy that made me feel extremely sorry for Lorian, though, unfortunately, even this did not bridge the gap between us.

Our paths haven't crossed again since that day, though when I think about it, I think about the past, about Nanuck and Simba, about Lorian, about the tangled Gothic heritage we all share. In my life, I have always had a great sense of friendship and, oddly, the friends I have chosen, and who have chosen me, have usually had an enormous feeling for family tradition. It is something I admire and, although it is not completely absent from my own family, it is perhaps that they are often such eccentric, talented and extraordinary people that they are individuals first and Franchettis second. It is possible that we have always lacked the strength of a patriarch, even though Papa was a powerful figure in life and, even in death, his voice has never stopped calling.

It was his native followers who eventually found his body after the explosion that killed him. He was buried by the sea in a Catholic monastery in Asmara in northern Ethiopia. His tomb has been worn by the desert winds and by the ravages of time, and I am sure it is in need of some attention. Soon I shall go – perhaps alone; perhaps not.

Oh yes, I did go to the theatre that night, though I can't remember what I saw. Afterwards, we went to a delightful restaurant and the stranger was sitting across the table from me.

'Can you pass the salt, please?' I asked.

He looked.

I looked.

'Can you pass the pepper, please ... ?'

Postscript

So, this is my life, well, a small part of it: cycles revolving and returning, as indeed they should, new horizons, but always a constant and eternal contact with those precious friends who have always been there, people who for me have a value beyond price, the bedrock of all that has ever been important to me.

It is presumptuous of a woman like me to try to write about herself, particularly as there have been many times when I felt an enormous cry building up inside me which I have never been able to express. I would have liked to have written more about my father, a man who helped to make history, and about my eccentric and complicated family, but, despite my faults, I was asked to write a book about me – a puzzle even to myself, a woman who, far from feeling that it is time to look back and reflect, finds that life is just beginning. Thus far, I have only glanced to right and left, never backwards and never too far forwards.

'Tomorrow is another day' has always been my motto and even in the most hysterical and dramatic situations, I can never stop myself from being secretly and irresponsibly an optimist.

My story does not contain any messages. There is so much more that I would have liked to say, but this book is like me – I can never fully express or project my feelings. I do not know what I would make of the woman revealed in these pages if I had just bought this book out of the blue. I have tried to be honest, perhaps even too honest. My feelings may appear to be no more than skin deep, but if you read between the lines, you will find a peephole through which you will see all the depths and fears and emotions I have tried to conceal.

About the Author

The daughter of Baron Raimondo Franchetti, the noted Italian explorer, Afdera Fonda grew up amid the Venetian aristocracy. It was at a party in Rome that she first met Henry Fonda, whom she married in 1957. Mrs. Fonda currently lives in London, where she works for an Anglo-Italian business and as an interviewer for the magazine *Speak Out*.

In the preparation of *Never Before Noon*, Afdera Fonda was assisted by journalist Clifford Thurlow, who is the author of many published articles and stories and co-author of *Carol Comes Home*, the autobiography of actress Carol White.